Geoffrey Chaucer

Tales from Chaucer in Prose

Geoffrey Chaucer

Tales from Chaucer in Prose

ISBN/EAN: 9783744689779

Printed in Europe, USA, Canada, Australia, Japan

Cover: Foto ©Thomas Meinert / pixelio.de

More available books at **www.hansebooks.com**

TALES

FROM

CHAUCER

IN PROSE.

DESIGNED CHIEFLY FOR THE USE OF YOUNG PERSONS.

BY

CHARLES COWDEN CLARKE,

AUTHOR OF 'THE RICHES OF CHAUCER' 'SHAKESPEARE CHARACTERS'
'MOLIÈRE CHARACTERS' ETC.

SECOND EDITION, CAREFULLY REVISED.

The Arms of Geoffry Chaucer.

Illustrated with Fourteen Wood Engravings.

LONDON:
C. LOCKWOOD & CO., 7 STATIONERS'-HALL COURT
1870.

LONDON: PRINTED BY
SPOTTISWOODE AND CO., NEW-STREET SQUARE
AND PARLIAMENT STREET

CONTENTS.

	PAGE
DEDICATION	v
ADVERTISEMENT	xi
MEMORIAL OF CHAUCER	1
PROLOGUE TO THE CANTERBURY TALES	59
THE KNIGHT'S TALE: Palamon and Arcite	91
THE MAN OF LAW'S TALE: The Lady Constance	142
THE WIFE OF BATH'S TALE: Court of King Arthur	172
THE CLERK'S TALE: Griselda	187
THE SQUIRE'S TALE: Cambuscan	224
THE PARDONER'S TALE: The Death-Slayers	254
THE PRIORESS'S TALE: The Murdered Child	272
THE NUN'S PRIEST'S TALE: The Cock and the Fox	282
THE CANON-YEOMAN'S TALE: The Alchymist	302
THE COOK'S TALE: Gamelin	324

ADDRESS

TO

MY YOUNG READERS.

I HAVE endeavoured to put these Tales, written by one of the finest poets that ever lived, into modern language, and as easy prose as I could, without at the same time destroying the poetical descriptions, and strong natural expressions of the author. My object in presenting them in this new form was, first, that you might become wise and good, by the example of the sweet and kind creatures you will find described in them: secondly, that you might derive improvement by the beautiful writing;—(for I have been careful to use the language of CHAUCER whenever I thought it not too antiquated for modern and young readers :) and, lastly, I hoped to excite in you an ambition to read these same stories in their original poetical dress, when you shall have become so far acquainted with your own language, as to understand, without much difficulty, the old, and now almost forgotten terms.

I can promise those among you, who possess an ear for the harmony of verse, that when you come to read the compositions of this great poet, you will then feel how much they have lost, by being reduced to my dull prose :— although I have laboured to render my narratives as much like *poetical* prose as I was able; and, more particularly, to give them the air of ancient writing, newly dressed up. And I believe I may say, that I have in no instance omitted to introduce a beautiful or natural thought, when I could do so with ease and propriety, and without interfering with the quick progress of the story.

In the original Tales are many long discussions, which you would find uninteresting at any age; and there are, also, quaint or curious expressions, which would not be pleasing to your differently educated ears :—these I have omitted altogether, except when I felt that they would preserve the old character of the narration, and not be too old-fashioned to be misunderstood by you.

Some of Chaucer's Tales, also, are of so coarse and indelicate a character, as to be unfit for perusal; and this circumstance, more perhaps than his antiquated dialect, has contributed to raise so great a prejudice against his writings in general, in the minds of parents and instructors, as altogether to prohibit their being read by young persons: but, as a distaste for vice will assuredly keep pace with our love of virtue, so a well regulated and delicately instructed mind will no more crave after and feed upon impure writings, than a healthy and natural stomach will desire and select carrion or dirt.

DRYDEN and POPE have recomposed some of Chaucer's Tales in modern verse; and, in doing so, have failed to maintain that very simple and vivid mode of description which renders his poetry so charming to those who feel, as they read, what he wished to describe: I need not, therefore, recommend you to refrain from reading any modern *verse* translation of him, but to cultivate your taste for old poetry, till you are able to read his as freely as you do the present volume.

The following sentence from Mr. LAMB's preface to his prose tales from the plays of SHAKSPEARE—a book every one of you should read—will explain all I would say upon the present occasion.

'Faint and imperfect images,' he says, 'they must be called, (of the original Dramas) 'because the beauty of his (Shakspeare's) 'language is too frequently destroyed by the 'necessity of changing many of his excellent 'words into words far less expressive of his

'true sense, to make it read something like
'prose; and even in some places, where his
'verse is given unaltered, as, hoping from its
'simple plainness, to cheat the young readers
'into a belief that they are reading prose, yet
'still, his language being transplanted from
'its own natural soil and wild poetic garden,
'it must want much of its native beauty.'

May you, in reading these pages, experience half the pleasure that the writing of them has afforded

Your Countryman and Friend,

THE AUTHOR.

ADVERTISEMENT.

THE ADULT READER (should I be honoured with such), who can scarcely fail to discern an abrupt stiffness in the construction of the sentences in the following Tales, will bear in mind the complicated difficulties I have had to contend with, in retaining, as much as possible, Chaucer's antique quaintness and distinctive character; in avoiding his repetitions, and yet in incorporating every nervous expression which constitutes the great charm of his graphic descriptions.

The task I proposed to myself, was, to render my translations literal with the original; to preserve their antique fashion; and withal to give them a sufficiently modern air to interest the young reader. I was to be at one and the same time 'modernly antique,' prosaically poetic, and comprehensively concise. He only will appreciate my frequent perplexities who shall attempt the same task,—observing the same restrictions.

A MEMORIAL OF GEOFFRY CHAUCER.

CONSIDERABLE AGITATION has been excited by the biographers of Chaucer regarding the station that his family held in society. One, —Leland, says he was of noble stock; another, —Pitts, that he was the son of a knight; Speght says that his father was a vintner; and Hearne, that he was a merchant. The question, therefore, is a doubtful one; though for the following reasons we may rationally infer that he was of gentle birth. First; he was bred at both universities; he had travelled through several of the countries of Europe, and was a student in the Temple. Secondly, the circumstance of his being appointed to the office of serving as one of the king's pages warrants the conclusion that would be drawn of the respectability of his family; seeing that in those days, birth was minutely required to qualify a person for the station of page to the king. Thirdly, his connection by marriage with the family of John of Gaunt, the great Duke of Lancaster; the match being not merely sanctioned, but recommended by that proud nobleman, considerably strengthens the argument. Yet, after all the discussions that have been expended upon this not very important point, worthy men of his own time, and men of all subsequent ages who have enquired into his life and writings, unite in the opinion that he possessed an extraordinary talent, and a noble and incorruptible nature:—these qualities form the true aristocracy of humanity, and they are the only ones indeed worthy of a moment's consideration. His genius, his sensibility, and his refinement, (allowing for the age in which he lived), his generous deportment while in adversity and exile; his independence of principle, and steadiness of attachment; all exhibit the true gentleman, whatever may have been his father's worldly occupation.

The sirname of our poet is evidently of French origin, the old Norman word *Chaucier*, or *Chaussier*, signifying a shoemaker. The word too, as applied to the article of dress, must have been commonly used during his life; for, in the translation of the Gospel by Mark by Richard of Hampole, the hermit, who died in 1394, the following verse, 'There cometh one mightier than I after me, the latchet of whose shoes I am not worthy to stoop down and unloose,' is thus rendered:—
' A stalworther than I schal come eftar me, of whom I am not worthi downfallande, or knelande, to louse the thwonge of his CHAWCERS.' An ancestor, however, of the poet's, and probably the founder of his family in England, was a *Knight*, and came over with William the Conqueror, his name appearing in the roll of Battle Abbey.

This father of English poetry was born in the second year of the reign of Edward III., 1328, and certainly in London, notwithstanding the contradictory accounts of his biographers; since he himself, who must be the surest authority upon this point, when speaking of the troubles which were occurring in that city, says, 'The City of London, that is to me so dear and sweet, in which I was forth-grown; —and more kindly love have I to that place than to any other in earth, (as every kindly creature hath full appetite to that place of his kindly ingendure).'

The earliest account we have of Chaucer is, that he was entered a student of the University of Cambridge, of which college, however, no record exists, — none, at least, has hitherto been discovered. But from the very accurate description he has given of the distinct locality of the place in his humorous tale of the Miller of Trompington, Clare Hall, or Scholar, or Solere Hall (for Speght pronounces them all to be one and the same), may have been the college of which he was entered. Here at the age of eighteen he wrote his poem of the 'Court of Love.' From Cambridge he went to Oxford, but to which college is again as much a matter of conjecture as the former place of his abode. Here he completed his studies, and became, says his biographer, Leland, 'a ready logician, a smooth rhetorician, a pleasant poet, a grave philosopher, an ingenious mathematician, and a holy divine.'

Being thus accomplished, he travelled into France, Holland, and the Low Countries; and upon his return home, entered himself of the Inner Temple, where he studied the municipal laws of the land. Shortly after he had begun to turn his mind to this branch of learning, his lustrous talents made him known at the court of Edward III., a prince as eminent for his patronage of genius as for his romantic valour. In this gay region of chivalry, mirth and gallantry, surrounded by wit and beauty, he started upon the full career of life: his age, the prime of manhood, (nearly thirty,) and person of just proportion, with a fair and beautiful complexion, full and red lips, and a graceful and dignified carriage; to crown which attractions may be added his newly-fledged renown as a love-poet, all gave him the advantage over any competitors. A handsome and modest young poet moving about a gallant court, is a beautiful picture for the mind to contemplate.

His first preferment was to that of king's page, at a yearly salary of twenty marks—no mean stipend at that period; this act was followed by appointment to the office of gentleman of the king's privy chamber, with an additional gratuity of twenty marks; and shortly after we find him promoted to be shield-bearer to the king, a post of signal honour, since, by the fulfilment of its duties he was brought in immediate vicinage to the royal person, and upon occasions of victory was rewarded with military honours.

In this gay sphere he was patronized and courted by John of Gaunt, who manifested a more than ordinary esteem for him, and for whom, in celebration of certain events in his life, he wrote 'The Book of the Duchess,' 'The Complaint of the Black Knight,' and 'The Dreame of Chaucer:' also, by the lovely Lady Blanche, his duchess, at whose request he wrote 'La Prière de Notre Dame:' by the womanly and heroic Queen Philippa; and, lastly, by the

Lady Margaret, Countess of Pembroke, and daughter of the king, who appears to have justly appreciated his extraordinary genius, for she is said to have frequently complimented him upon his poems, as well as to have excited him to familiar and intellectual intercourse, seeing that she would rally him upon his modest and silent habit.

The Duchess Blanche retained in her service Catherine, the daughter of Sir Payne, or Pagan Rouet, a native of Hainault, and guien king at arms for that territory. This lady married Sir Hugh Swinford, Knight at Lincoln, who dying shortly after their union, the duke and duchess renewed their protection, appointing her governess of their children. Lady Swinford, after the death of the Duchess Blanche, became the duke's mistress, and subsequently his third wife. She was a woman so eminent for beauty, that the circumstance was recorded upon her tomb in the cathedral of old St. Paul. Her sister Philippa was recommended to Chaucer by the Duchess Blanche, as one with whom he might advantageously contract a matrimonial alliance, and by this union it was that the poet became allied to the royal family of England.

About the period of his marriage he received another proof of royal favour in the grant of a pitcher of wine, to be furnished to him daily; and this was quickly followed by his being appointed comptroller of the customs for wool, woolfels, and hides, with an especial clause subjoined to the patent, that the duties of the office should be performed in person, and even that the accounts should be written with his own hand. This proviso on the part of Edward has been sneered at, and apparently not without reason, by those who uphold the system of creating places of emolument for the sole purpose of maintaining persons who it is not intended should fulfil the duties connected with them. If the entire labour of an office be performed by hirelings, these should either derive the whole benefit attaching to it, or the salary of the ostensible and inefficient clerk becomes an absolute injustice inflicted upon the people who are required to raise that salary. Chaucer was no drone in the common hive; he filled this situation with unimpeached honour and integrity, and at the time when places of the same description, in the old age and weakness of the king, were farmed out, and the people compelled to pay for services not performed, no shade of imputation for such unworthiness attaches to this poet's memory. No one, as he says of himself, could 'speak evil of his administration;' also, that he 'never defouled his conscience for any manner of deed.' This life is too short, and too full of sorrows, not of our own seeking, for us to add to their number by acts of baseness and dishonour.

In the forty-seventh year of the poet's age, and the forty-ninth of the king's reign, he received from Edward a grant of the lands and body of the son of Sir Edmond Staplegate, in the county of Kent, in ward, for which he was subsequently paid one hundred and four pounds; and in the following year the royal patron bestowed upon him, by the title of 'Dilectus armiger noster,' (our beloved knight) the sum of seventy-one pounds four shillings and sixpence, being a forfeit of custom dues levied upon a citizen of London for non-payment upon a quantity of wool. These casual benefits, together with his permanent offices of emolument, contributed to render him a very wealthy man; Speght indeed, one of his historians, states that he had at this time almost one thousand pounds per annum. He himself, in the 'Testament of Love,' acknowledges his advanced fortunes, and says, ' I had comfort to be in that plight, that both profit were to me *and my friends*;' an unconscious insinuation on his part that he was not a selfish character. Again he avows that, 'in dignity of office he made gathering of those goods, and had a fair parcel for the time, in furthering of his sustenance, riches sufficient to waive necessity, dignity to be reverenced in worship, power to keep from enemies;' so that, 'he seemed to shine in glory of renown, as manhood asketh in men.'

The Duke of Lancaster, with all his noble qualities, was a man of inordinate pride and ambition; and, as is usually the result, when this quality once takes possession of the mind, he did not permit the delicacies of honour and justice to obstruct the accomplishment of his desires. Upon the death of his elder brother, the Black Prince, he fixed a steady and craving eye upon the crown, omitting no available means to secure to himself the succession, in the event of the demise of the aged king his father. And indeed, so passionately was he in love with dominion, that, rather than not be a king, he was content to ally himself with the disreputable Peter the Cruel, connecting himself with a ruined and disjointed family, by marrying the daughter Constance; and this for the sole purpose of succeeding to the title of King of Castile. In order, however, to realize the darling object of his ambition — the inheritance of the English crown, he moved every engine in his power to lessen that of the established clergy, knowing that they were opposed to his views, and strenuous for the legitimate succession. He therefore espoused the doctrines and cause of the first great ecclesiastical reformer, Wickliffe, industriously exasperating against the regular clergy the popular discontent, which had at this early period become prevalent and inveterate, by reason of their disgusting appetite for obtaining possession of all the places of trust and honour. The following may be received as a sample of the justice of the nobles' and people's discontent. 'The Archbishop of Canterbury was Lord Chancellor; the Bishop of Bath and Wells was Lord Treasurer; the Archdeacon of Lincoln, Privy Seal; David Weller, Parson of Summersham, Master of the Rolls; ten beneficed Priests, Civilians, Masters in Chancery; William Mulse, Dean of St. Martin's-le-Grand, Chamberlain of the Exchequer, Privy Purse, and Master of the Jewel House; William Ashton, Archdeacon of Northampton, Chancellor of the Exchequer; William Dighton, Prebendary of St. Martin's, Clerk of the Privy Seal; John de Troy, Priest, Treasurer of Ireland; Snatch, Parson of Oundle, Master of the Wardrobe; John Newham, Parson of Fenny Stanton, one of the Chamberlains of the Exchequer; John Rousbic, Parson of Harwick, Comptroller and Surveyor of the King's Buildings; and Thomas Britingham, Parson of Ashby, Treasurer for Guienne, and Marshal of Calais.'[1] Chaucer,

---

[1] Life by Urry.

no doubt from an honest impulse of opposition to the same establishment, aided also by an interested desire to promote the views of his patron, became involved in his intrigues, and essentially helped forward the cause of the reformation by his formidable attacks upon the weak and corrupt branches of the ecclesiastical government. His innate love of justice and liberality, however, would not suffer him to become an undiscriminating and malignant opposer; if therefore he lashed the whole body of the clergy in the 'Plowman's Tale,' and in his treatise entitled 'Jack Upland,' he has rarely omitted availing himself of the opportunity of eulogizing such individuals as were worthy of their calling; a beautiful instance of this occurs in his character of the Poor Parson in the Prologue to the Canterbury Tales. Godwin, however, is of opinion that the 'Plowman's Tale,' and 'Jack Upland,' were not written by Chaucer; but that, 'both in language and sentiments, they appear to belong to a later period.'[1]

But to return to the proceedings of our

[1] 'Life of Chaucer,' vol. ii. 4to. p. 402.

poet's patron, the Duke of Lancaster. Although he numbered many partisans among the nobility, and was tacitly countenanced by the king himself (who favoured the doctrines of Wickliffe) in his opposition to the clergy, the sagacious old monarch was nevertheless not blind to the motive which had roused his son to that action; he therefore promptly resolved upon the wise and just course of obviating future discord and commotion, by declaring Richard of Bourdeaux, son of the Black Prince, heir to the crown, to the no small envy and mortification of the Duke of Lancaster, whose restless ambition and jealousies, so far from being quenched by the decision, kept the young monarch and his court in perpetual excitement and uneasiness.

The next public employment in which we find Chaucer engaged, is that of ambassador, having been sent out to France in conjunction with the Earl of Huntingdon and Sir Richard Sturry to negotiate a match between the daughter of the French king, and the young Prince of Wales, afterwards Richard II. The mission, however, terminated only in obtaining a prolongation of a truce between the two countries which had been infringed on the part of the French, who had infested our coasts, disturbing the course of trade.

Richard II. having succeeded to the crown of his grandfather, June 21, 1377; among other acts in the first year of his reign, confirmed to our poet the grant of twenty marks per annum made by the late king; also the grant of the daily pitcher of wine: and in the following year he is discovered under the immediate protection of Richard with regard to his lands and possessions, probably from some embarrassment in his circumstances. Speght infers that his troubles arose from his having sided with the common people in their political contentions, but that era in his life had not yet occurred. Whether his troubles at this time arose from his disregard of economy, loss of patronage at court, or munificent spirit when engaged in foreign embassies, it would be difficult at this distant period to determine.

In the fourth year of the reign of Richard II., that prince confirmed to Chaucer and his wife Philippa the annuity grants that had been made to them. About the same time too the poet's son Thomas married Maud, daughter of Sir John Burghershe; she was one of the wealthiest heiresses of that time.

The opinions of Wickliffe that had for years been gathering heat and strength, now exploded in the rebellion under the celebrated Wat Tyler. The doctrines of the great reformer, however, were not uniformly propagated in the pure spirit of the heavenly promulgator of Christianity; for, one of Wickliffe's disciples, named Smith, was supported by men of substance and title, who always attended him armed. In their zeal for the cause therefore, Knighton, a mild writer of that time, says, that 'what they could not convince by reason, they terrified into opinion.' This Mahometan mode of propagating religion, however, does not attach to the head of the new sect; but the coarser-minded followers, as Tyler and his exasperated companions, wreaked their full vengeance upon the church dignitaries who fell under their power. They beheaded the Archbishop of

Canterbury,[1] and the prior of St. John's near Smithfield, (who was Lord Treasurer,) burning the fine priory itself, and sacked several abbeys; among others those of Bury and St. Albans. The oppressions of the government, it is true, were the chief cause of Wat Tyler's rebellion, but it must be remembered that churchmen constituted the majority of the governors; and though that unsuccessful rebel was doubtless guilty of many outrages, and innocent men suffered with guilty ones by the 'wild justice' of himself and followers, (the unfailing result of an injured and irritated people clutching the sword of administration,) yet, upon reading the terms he stipulated for on behalf of himself and fellow commoners, they will be found, in the main, so just and rational as to sanction the resistance of the governed in the event of their not being complied with.

Neither Chaucer nor any of the heads of the reforming party can be included in this rebellion, since the members of it made no

---

[1] See page 12.

exception in favour of the Duke of Lancaster, whose palace in the Savoy they burnt down. Our poet, indeed, it appears, ceased to take any prominent part in the new doctrines when he saw them and their authors abandoned by his patron; whose desertion of the cause bears date about the period that his hopes of success against the clergy for the furtherance of his own political views were dissipated. The part which Chaucer acted throughout this memorable struggle is somewhat difficult to be reconciled with great strength of mind and consistency, since in the 'Testament of Love' he acknowledges the real presence in the sacrament; and in his retractation renounces all he may have written detrimental to the interests of the Roman Catholic hierarchy. In a question of faith, a man is at full liberty, it is true, to change his opinions; but the doing so at the last period of life is not entitled to high consideration, when neither mind nor body can be in its full condition of elasticity. Retractation in a question of religious creed at such a moment must be lightly regarded by the philosophical mind;

indeed, at any period of life, till the pointed question of Pilate—'What is TRUTH?' be decided, it is of little more importance (always providing that the motive be pure and conscientious) than changing the fashion of one's garment; for to use the homely but apt illustration of Selden; 'one wears his doublet plain, and another slashed, but every man wears a doublet; so every man has a religion: we only differ about the trimmings.'

We now come to the period of the poet's adversity and troubles. In the year 1384, the Duke of Lancaster having been charged by a friar, named Latimer, with an attempt to murder the King, the informant was secretly assassinated by Lord Holl and others, under whose custody he was placed, before he could clear his charge. However this black act may reasonably compromise the innocence of the Duke, the historians and biographers of the period nevertheless agree in declaring the whole affair to have been a plot framed by his enemies; and the King, knowing the supple conscience of his infamous tool, Judge Tresilian, determined to bring him to trial. The

Duke knowing the danger in which he would be placed by trusting to the justice of his enemies with such a man at their head, stood upon his guard in the castle of Pontefract, till, by the mediation of the Dowager Princess of Wales, matters were arranged. His influence and interest, however, from this moment faded to a shadow, and when he deserted all his adherents and personal friends, and passed over sea, they, with the poet among the rest, began to experience the full weight of party animosity. The political opponents of the Duke had long watched their occasion for revenge, and when it arrived they made ample use of it. By every possible means they could devise they oppressed his adherents, while these in turn resorted to the common alternative of exciting popular commotions. In one instance Chaucer himself was not an unimportant engine. A man named John Comburton, or John of Northampton, a partisan of the Duke's, having been elected Mayor of London, made strong interest to be a second time returned to the office, upon the ground that he would exert himself to reform the abuses which had crept into the government of the corporation. The contest ran so strongly that the citizens broke out into open insurrection, and Chaucer being at that time Comptroller of the Customs, joined the party of Northampton. The riot, however, was quickly suppressed; one of the rioters was beheaded, the candidate Northampton taken into custody, and active search was made after our poet; but he had made his escape into Hainault, from whence he passed into France; and finding that the King was exerting every means to entrap him, he removed into Zealand. It appears from collateral circumstances, that his wife, Philippa, accompanied him in his exile. 'Prudence' (says Godwin) 'would have dictated their separation;'—not if she were mentally and personally worthy to be his wife. The principal reason for his avoiding apprehension was, because he had heard it was the determination of the court to make him betray the authors of and principal agents in the insurrection.

He had now become a wanderer upon the earth, dreading to see the face of a stranger, lest he should prove an emissary from the court of his own country to entrap him. Several accomplices in the riot had also followed the poet in his exile, and these he generously supported from his own reduced means; and, as he himself says, remained abroad and 'concealed their privitie longer than he should' for his own personal advantage; for his partisans at home had speedily made their peace with the government, by submission and acknowledgement of their offence: yet these with infinite baseness and ingratitude not only proceeded to blacken his character, but even contrived to cut off the remittance of his supplies. They let his apartments, and never accounted to him for the rent, and in short hoped to accomplish his death. He now deemed that farther maintenance of delicacy towards such partisans would be mere romance; he therefore determined upon returning home. We may here remark, as a strong corroboration in evidence of Chaucer's self-expatriation not having been altogether undertaken from selfish motives, but that he might screen his accomplices, the singular circumstance that during the whole period of his retirement his situation of comptroller was filled *by deputy;* indeed, when he was finally dismissed from office, neither Richard nor his ministers were the persons to offer him the indignity, but the celebrated Thomas of Woodstock, that King's bitter enemy, and for some time lord and master. He was therefore not wholly an exile in favour as well as in person, and he must have been certain that a voluntary confession and submission on his part would at least prove equally advantageous to him as to the other members of the insurrection who had not enjoyed the court favour. He did return—and had not long been home before he was arrested by an order from the King, and imprisoned, as it is supposed, in the Tower. Here he was subjected to a severe examination on the part of the council, with the design to draw from him the betrayal of his associates: he, however, evaded their object long, and with the utmost of his ingenuity, till they at length informed him that his only chance of obtaining the royal mercy was in exposing the secrets of his party. His tenacity of purpose now relaxed, and he disclosed all he knew, impeaching at the same time the persons who had been connected with him. This act in his life is the only one known, that has in any degree tainted his memory; yet is it not ot be dismissed without extenuation; and for this end we shall prefer availing ourselves of the cool, philosophical, and eloquent defence of Mr. Godwin, to any arguments that we could offer in behalf of one of the most eminent as well as most estimable beings on 'Fame's eternal bead-roll.'

'This, undoubtedly, is the circumstance in the life of Chaucer which conveys the most unfavourable impression of him to modern times. He stands here in the light of a person who accepted the confidence of a certain party; who, from the persuasion that they might safely trust him, was admitted into their secrets; who partook of their counsels, and shared their attempts; and who afterwards purchased his safety by betraying his associates. Nothing can justify such a conduct, but the supposition that the individual by whom it is adopted has been deluded into some project of an exceedingly criminal nature, that he is afterward led by his reflections to see it in its true enormity, and that no way remains to prevent the perpetration but by a judicial impeachment; such a situation is described in the person of Jaffier in Abbé St. Real's narrative of the conspiracy of Venice. In that case the treachery employed may be admitted to be commendable, and in some degree to atone for the weakness and guilt incurred by the accuser in the begining of the transaction.

'But the situation of Chaucer was by no means of this sort. The confederacy into which he had entered was probably a commendable one; and the end for which it had been formed had passed by, and the confederacy been dissolved, before Chaucer gave information respecting his associates.

'What, then, were the motives of his conduct? He has himself assigned one, in the indignation which he conceived against them. They had plotted to starve him, had cut off his supplies, and embezzled his income. He probably thought that no measures were to be kept with persons who had conducted themselves towards him so basely. He was impatient of being any longer accounted their ally. All that was resentful in his nature was stirred up at the thought of the treatment he had endured, and he felt as if it would be an offence against morality and human nature to suffer such villainy to go unpunished. These sentiments are undoubtedly congenial to the mind of a man deeply injured; and especially when the injury proceeds from those for whom he has sacrificed much, whom he has liberally assisted in their difficulties, and for his connection with whom he is even still suffering calamity and distress. Such sentiments may extenuate what is offensive in the conduct of Chaucer in this instance, but cannot justify it. He who pursues retribution for the offences of others should firmly refuse to obtain it by any sacrifice of the dignity and rectitude of his own character.

'Perhaps, however, Chaucer was influenced in his compliance with the importunities and threats of the administration, by a certain degree of timidity and irresolution. This is a very common feature of human character; and though it must be confessed to be a blemish, is not destructive of the fundamental principles of a virtuous temper. Chaucer, it may be, was inaccessible to the attacks of corruption; he boasts very loudly, in the performance we are considering, (the 'Testament of Love,') of his unimpeachable integrity in the execution of his functions as a servant of the crown. He was not easily intimidated, or induced, by calamity or fear, to turn aside from his course: he was for a considerable period faithful to his engagements with his associates, and, as he tells us, 'conceled their privitie longer than he should.' Such a man might be an excellent member of private and domestic society, a true patriot, and a genuine lover of mankind; he might be a stranger to the selfish passions, and to that mutability which is so pernicious to the best purposes of life; generous, tender, affectionate, warm-hearted, and charitable. With such endowments a man might have passed through life in twenty different stations, and not a speck of soil have fastened upon the whiteness of his actions; had not that single temptation occurred against which alone he was not proof, had not fortune maliciously conspired to direct her attacks against the only imperfect and vulnerable point in his nature.

'In estimating the morality of Chaucer's conduct on this occasion, it is also incumbent upon us to take into the account the length of his misfortunes and his imprisonment. From the documents and the reasonings we have produced it seems clearly to follow, that his confinement in the Tower endured for no less a period than three years. He had, perhaps, been an exile for two years previously to his imprisonment. He had passed through an accumulation of evils; starved for want of remittances abroad, and induced to sell the slender pittance which remained to him in the form of a pension, for subsistence. He whose resolution holds out during five years of calamity and distress, is no fickle and effeminate character. If Chaucer, who had witnessed the anarchy of his country, and the tragical scenes which were transacted almost in his presence, who had been reduced to barter his last resources for bread, and who saw an affectionate wife and a cherished offspring in danger to perish for want, felt at length subdued and willing to give up somewhat of the sternness of his virtue, we may condemn him as moralists, but we cannot fail in some degree to sympathise with feelings which make an essential part of our nature.

'One idea arises in this place which cannot fail to strike us as interesting and instructive. Chaucer tells us that his conduct in this instance involved him in a torrent of ill will, and brought upon him the charge of being false, lying, base, and ungrateful. It was principally to defend himself against these charges, that he composed his elaborate performance of the "Testament of Love."

'It is probable that the lapse of a single generation would have blotted out from the memory of his countrymen these censures upon the "father of English poetry." Who now appears as his accuser? Chaucer: Chaucer only. We have no evidence but what we draw from this production,—that he was ever concerned in the turmoils of the city, that he was an exile, a prisoner in the Tower, and that he was finally led by resentment or by terror to the dishonourable act of impeaching his confederates. Little did the poet think, when he sat down to make this laborious apology for his conduct, that he was hereby perpetuating an imputation, which, without his interference, Time was preparing to blot out for ever from the records of memory, while his poetical compositions were destined to render him dear to the lovers of the muse as long as the English language shall endure. How feeble and erroneous are the calculations of the wisest of mankind!' Shortly after this event, in the year 1389, he was appointed to the office of Clerk of the Works, at a salary of *two shillings* per day,—equivalent to about six hundred and fifty pounds of modern money. The duty attendant upon his commission was to 'superintend the erection, repair, and embellishment of the King's mansions, parks, and domains.'[1]

It has been seen that by the retirement of the Duke of Lancaster from the country, our poet had almost wholly lost that patronage which he had mainly derived from the political influence of his powerful friend, and that he

---

[1] Godwin's 'Life of Chaucer,' vol. ii. 4to. edition.

had also, from the same cause, become exposed to the rage of his enemies. These had multiplied since his late confession in the Tower. The conscience of the Duke had also upbraided him on account of his disreputable connection with Lady Swinford; he therefore resorted to the conventional mode of expiating his fault by separating himself from her. This proceeding multiplied the sum of Chaucer's perplexities, and naturally; for being connected by marriage with the sister of that lady, he was not merely deprived of those numerous services which a woman who possesses any influence over the mind or affections of her lord is always enabled to render to her relations and friends; but her very state of desertion afforded his opponents an additional means of triumph. This double abandonment on the part of the Duke (that of his mistress and adherents) admits, however, of defence upon both points; upon the one, that he afterwards made ample restitution to an amiable and worthy woman for the false position in which he had placed her in society, by legally making her his wife; and on the other, that he had passed over into Castile for the purpose of claiming his right of succession to that crown. His success in this expedition appears to have been various and unequal; for although he failed in the main object of his attempt, that of being created king, yet he provided for his daughters; the one succeeding to be Queen of Castile, and the other Queen of Portugal. Like a sagacious warrior and politician both, he amply indemnified himself for his disappointment in the chief object of his ambition, by securing the next advantage to be drawn from his expedition—the accomplishment of wealth. Contemporary historians relate that he was attended on his return home by an accumulation of treasure that loaded forty-seven mules. His return, and the prosperous state of his revenue, gave new hopes to the party attached to him: his credit at court also had risen with his swollen fortune; so much so indeed, that the King, in full parliament assembled, created him Duke of Aquitaine, and commissioned him to go and preside over that fine principality.

During the absence of Lancaster, Chaucer

had carefully secluded himself from the world in the lovely retreat of Woodstock, since become an object of deep interest from that circumstance, and exalted into equal celebrity with the Mantua of Virgil, the Vaucleuse of Petrarch, and the Valle delle Dame of Boccacio. Few persons not wholly indifferent to the charm and sentiment of association, would pass Blenheim without turning their steps to this Mecca of our poet, there to offer the simple homage of admiration and gratitude due to extraordinary genius. Here may still be traced in his lines, as by a chart, the walks he was accustomed to take in the prime of the day, when the sun looked 'ruddy and brode' through the morning vapour; when the dew 'like silver shining' was upon the 'sweet grass,' and his beloved daisy was beginning to unfold its pinky lashes. Here is still the rivulet by which he coasted, with its water 'clear as beryl or crystal,' and the 'walled park of greene stone:'—here is the 'fresh hawthorn in white motley, that so sweet doeth ysmell;' and the birds are here cropping the 'small buds and round blossoms;' and the 'little well under the hill, with its quick streams and cold, and the gold gravel, and the banks environing, soft as velvet.' How exquisite are these rural associations with the mind and habits of a great poet, compared with those of the artificial world! Who in thinking of Chaucer connects him with the comptrollership of the Customs, or as page to Edward III.? yet these employments, with all their temporal benefits, brought with them much labour and anxiety; while the beneficent spirit of nature rewarded him during life with untroubled calm and happiness for his devotion at her shrine, and after death with a crown of glory as fresh and vivid as the recurring flowers that she sprinkles over her green lap.

In this retreat he wrote (or perhaps completed) his learned 'Treatise on the Astrolabe,' which he compiled for the use of his younger son, Lewis, then only ten years of age, but who was nevertheless so far advanced in learning as to desire his father's knowledge of the principles of astronomy.

About four years after this point in the history of our poet, his great patron returned home, and made that restitution to Lady Swinford already alluded to. The union in the first instance gave high offence, it appears, to the ladies connected with the royal family; but the good sense, placable demeanour, and unaffected humility of their new relation, so quickly smoothed the asperities of the whole court, that the King carried her with the Duke over to France when he married the daughter of the French King, young Isabel, his second consort, whom, on account of her slender age, he placed under the education of this very Duchess of Lancaster.

The change of affairs that at this period had occurred in the family of Chaucer proved of instantaneous advantage to himself. The King renewed the grant of twenty marks per annum, bestowed by his grandfather, Edward III., and which in his distress the poet had been compelled to dispose of.

In the following year we find him in the receipt of a grant of a pipe of wine annually, to be delivered from the Customs of the port of London by the chief butler, his son Thomas having been appointed to that office

But these gleams of sun-favour again became suddenly clouded by the death of his patron and brother-in-law, John of Gaunt. The loss of this good friend, and to whom he was sincerely attached, from the ties of gratitude as well as from personal motives of respect and admiration, (for he was a prince possessing many noble and generous qualities,) so deeply affected Chaucer, that we find him again withdrawing from public life and wholly retiring to Donnington Castle, a noble estate (presented to him by the Duke) situated near to the town of Newberry, at a short distance from the high road. As every place of residence connected with our poet must be acceptable to the reader, we give the following account of this mansion by one of his biographers. 'At present there is nothing to be seen of this ancient structure but what raises horror and concern: a battered gateway with two towers, and some small part of the shattered walls, being all the remains thereof. The grounds about it and the ruins of it are choked with brambles and overrun

Gateway to Donnington Castle, the last country residence of Chaucer.

with ivy: but lest the place of its situation should in a few years more be forgot, I shall, as plainly as I can, describe it. It lies half a mile to the right of Spinhamland, (the ancient Spina of Antonius,) a mile beyond Newberry, on the same side. As you go from London you pass over the river Kennet to the village of Dunnington, from which there is a pretty steep but pleasant ascent through a lane to a hill under the castle, where stands a seat formerly belonging to the Countess of Sandwich: from hence arises the castle-hill, very steep, and not unlike that whereon the observatory stands at Greenwich; and from this hill there is a very fine prospect of several counties. On the back of the castle are level grounds, woodlands, and enclosures. The castle itself stands in a pleasant park, in which there was a famous oak, called Chaucer's oak; under which, as tradition taught, he wrote several poems. Mr. Evelyn gives a particular account of this tree, and says there were three of them planted by Chaucer: the king's oak, the queen's oak, and Chaucer's oak.'[1] The one which *he*

---

[1] Bell's edition of Chaucer, vol. i. Life; p. 45.

himself planted cannot of course be *the* oak under which 'tradition teaches that he wrote several poems;' his residence at Donnington Castle not having exceeded two or three years.

During his abode in this retreat the great revolution occurred, which placed upon the throne the son of his brother-in-law, John of Gaunt, young Henry of Lancaster, better known as Henry IV. Although such an event in a political point of view could not have been an unwelcome one to Chaucer, yet it is gratifying to reflect upon his conduct upon the occasion. We do not find that with the worldling and courtier's insincerity he pressed forward to congratulate the successful usurper; or, which is infinitely worse, that he chuckled over the reverses and miseries of his late kind and generous, if weak, benefactor; yet this execrable baseness attaches to the memory of our poet's friend, Gower, who, with the callous selfishness that not unfrequently accompanies a blind old age, spurned the fallen patron through whose munificence he had enjoyed a larger share of favour than had fallen to the lot of Chaucer himself. We may conceive how that generous and noble soul must have revolted at such miserable ingratitude in a brother poet and friend.

During the first year of his reign, however, Henry confirmed to Chaucer, and of his own free will, the annuities he had enjoyed from his former master; and in addition, partly from admiration of his genius, and partly on account of his near alliance to, and ancient friendship with his own father, he confirmed to him during the term of his life, an annuity of forty marks per annum.

The short period in which he survived the dethroning of Richard was mainly occupied in arranging his worldly affairs, which had been thrown into disorder; for all the public acts of that unhappy monarch were, after his deposition, annulled. Chaucer was, therefore, compelled to leave the quiet of Donnington, and plunge into the turmoil of business, a change of habit that few aged men could encounter with impunity—to the poet, who was stooping under the weight of years, it proved fatal. His residence in London (whether at the present period of his life, or not, is uncertain) was at the sign of the Red Rose, in Palace Yard, Westminster, on the site where Henry VII.'s Chapel now stands. In the full enjoyment of his clear faculties, but with an exhausted frame, he died on the 25th of October, 1400, in the 72nd year of his age.

As a proof of the activity and soundness of his perceptive faculties, he composed a few verses 'upon his death-bed, when he was in great anguish,' exposing the vanity of human wishes and endeavours, entitled 'Gode Counsaile of Chaucer;' and beginning 'Fly from the press,[1] and dwell with sothfastness.'[2]

He descended to his grave in the fullness of a high reputation as an extraordinary genius, and a generous and noble-minded man. He was buried in the great south aisle of Westminster Abbey—that quarter now so well known under the name of 'Poet's Corner.' Some writers have described that he was first laid in the Cloister, and afterwards removed; but Caxton, (who may be relied on as an

---

[1] Crowd. [2] Truth.

authority,) in his edition of the poet's works, states that he was buried in the Abbey church of Westminster, before the chapel of St. Bennet (or Benedict). This account was written before the removal, alluded to above, took place.

There appears to be a considerable difficulty in ascertaining the exact depository of his remains; nor indeed does it seem clear that the present monument of him was erected over or even near to that spot; moreover, it is not the original monument placed to his memory, which Speght says contained the following verses,

'Galfridus Chaucer, vates et fama poesis
Maternæ, hac sacra sum tumulatus humo;'

'I, Geoffry Chaucer, the Bard and glory of my mother country, was buried in this sacred ground.'

but was erected by a Mr. Nicholas Brigham, of Oxford, in the year 1556, a gentleman who enthusiastically honoured the memory of the poet. Upon this monument, as represented at the conclusion of the present memoir, he caused Chaucer's portrait to be painted from that which was in Occleve, his scholar's book, and added the inscription, the whole of which is now obliterated. It is to be hoped that there is truth in the report recently circulated, of a proposal having been made to restore this monument to its originally perfect state.

M. S.

Qui fuit Anglorum vates ter maximus olim,
Galfridus Chaucer conditur hoc tumulo:
Annum si quæras Domini, si tempora vitæ,
Ecce notæ subsunt quæ tibi cuncta notunt.

25 Octobris 1400.

Ærumnarum requies mors.

N. Brigham hos fecit Musarum nomine sumptus.

1556.

TRANSLATION.

He who was the most eminent of English poets—Geoffry Chaucer—lies beneath this tomb: if you require the term of his life, and the year, the record is subscribed, which will inform you all.

25 October, 1400.

Death is the repose of sorrows.

N. Brigham placed these, in the Muses' name, at his own cost.

1556.

Around the edge of the tomb the following verses are said to have been inscribed, now also obliterated.

> 'Si rogites quis eram, forsan te fama docebit;
> Quod si fama negat, mundi quia gloria transit,
> Hæc monumenta lege.'

'Should you enquire who I was, mayhap Fame will instruct you; but if Fame refuse, (since the glory of this world passeth away,) read this monument.'

The person of Chaucer was of middle stature, in advanced years, inclining to corpulency. In his journey with the Pilgrims to Canterbury, mine host of the Tabard takes occasion to jest with him upon this point;—comparing both their persons, he says;

> 'Now ware you sirs, and let this man have place;
> He in the waist is shaped as well as I;
> This were a poppet in armès to embrace,' &c.

His face was full and smooth, betokening regular good health, and a serene and cheerful frame of mind. His complexion was fair, verging towards paleness: his hair was of a dusky yellow, short and thin; that of his beard grew, or rather perhaps it was fashioned into a forked shape, and its colour was wheaten. He had an expansive and marble-like forehead, fair and unwrinkled; his eyes constantly tended towards the ground—a habit he has likewise given occasion in the host to notice:

> 'What man art thou, (quoth he,)
> That lookest as thou wouldest find a hare;
> For ever on the ground I see thee stare.'

The general expression of his countenance combined a mixture of animation, of lurking, good natured satire, of unruffled serenity, sweetness, and close thought. As in the above passages from his great poem we are let into a lively portrait of some of his personal peculiarities, so in the 'Testament of Love' as perfect an idea of his actions and manner in conversation are farther displayed; so that one may almost fancy oneself in the prison with him, listening to his discourses on philosophy. 'The downcast look, (says Urry,) the strict attention, the labouring thought, the hand waving for silence, the manner of address in speaking, the smooth familiar way of arguing, the respectful way of starting his objections, and, in short, every expression in that dispute, figures a lively image of him in the mind of the reader.'

His features, as in most instances of sincere and transparent natures, were an index of his temper, and this comprised a mixture of the lively, grave, and modest. Yet was the gaiety of his disposition more prominent in his writings than in his general demeanour, which, it may be, was repressed by his modesty. This bashfulness it was, which gave occasion to the Countess of Pembroke often to banter him; declaring, that his absence was preferable to his conversation, since the latter was naught, on account of his reserve and distant respect; whereas, when he was away from her, the chance was, he might be preparing some composition to afford her delight. His behaviour with the pilgrims is uniformly in keeping with this habit of silence and seclusion. He scarcely appears in person, and when called upon for his tale, endeavours to avoid the task by singing a ballad; the host, however, protesting against this departure from the general compact, his own story (or rather discourse) is one of the least interesting in the whole series.

His youth was not altogether free from the indiscretions natural to a man surrounded by the beauty and wit of an admiring court; that he was not even tainted, however, with the vacillation and heartlessness of the mere debauchee and man of pleasure, is evident from the single circumstance of his steady courtship of the lady who ultimately became his wife, which continued for eight years. Besides, his constant behaviour towards women, and his exalted admiration of them, at once exempt him from being a coarse or common intriguer. Many of his tales are questionable in their morality, (and these in after life he repented having penned,) but it is strongly doubtful, (coarse as they are,) whether they would so surely sap the structure of a well-educated young mind as many productions of some modern writers, and which are nevertheless found in almost every book-case in the kingdom.

During his relaxations from the duties of public business, he continually retired to his study. Reading, indeed, was his chief delight, as appears, by his own confession, in the introduction to his 'Dreame,' and to the 'Legend of Good Women.' He preferred it to every amusement, with the exception of a morning walk in May-tide. He lived almost exclusively in his own world of meditation, never interfering, as he says of himself, in the concerns of others. He was temperate and regular in his diet; he 'arose with the lark, and lay down with the lamb:' hence the marvellous truth and freshness of his early morning pictures, not inferior to the celebrated 'Castle Landscape' of Rembrandt; and this is the most perfect representation of a morning twilight that, perhaps, ever was painted.

The career of Chaucer, from whichever point we may view it, assumes a character greatly elevated above that of ordinary men. He was a poet, a philosopher, an astronomer, a logician, a linguist, a politician, a theologian, a humanist, a gentleman in the modern acceptation of the term, and a virtuous man. His conduct as a man holding a public office stands unimpeached for integrity. He was a gentleman,—for he was the universal theme of admiration in a refined court—particularly by the women, and they rarely err in making a correct estimate of a man's temper and habits. He was a humanist, for he has ever at hand an apology for the frailties of our nature;—above all, when he would atone for the lapses of the most responsible and the least excused of our race—the women. Proofs of this may be seen scattered over all his works, but it shines forth most conspicuously in his divine poem of Troilus and Cressida, where his pleadings for the error of that too light heart may without profaneness be ranked with the conduct of HIM, who bade her sister delinquent to 'go and sin no more.'

In his public capacity, as a politician and theological controversialist, he appears to have been an opponent of abuses rather from a spirit of party than from an active principle of justice, or from consciousness of the truth, for we find that in the one instance he aided a body of insurgents because they were the partizans of his patron; and in the other he withdrew his opposition to the priesthood when he found that the Duke himself no longer made it a handle for promoting his ambitious views with regard to the succession. Indeed we do not find it confirmed that he sided with Wickliffe upon points of faith or doctrine, but in exposing the abuses of his mother church. He was a *reformer*, not a *seceder*; he would have restored the catholic worship to its primitive purity, but he would not have removed one stone of the fabric. This opinion is borne out by his confession of faith, wherein he subscribes to the whole rubric. Wickliffe applied his battering-ram at one of its main corner-stones—transubstantiation. For one of lively imagination, strong sensitiveness, and of devotedness to the gentler luxuries and enjoyments of life, Chaucer was an active and steady partizan in the cause of reform; but a temperament like his was not calculated to make thorough work in a contest with the knitted phalanx of corruption. Such as he, are not the wedge to split the 'gnarred and stubby tree' of a full-grown opinion. The man of imagination is seldom calculated to maintain an up-hill struggle in the cause of reform; and the most unflinching and uncompromising soldiers, whether for an opinion or for hire, are not always men of excessive imagination; the poets have not been at any time the stubbornest of patriots. MILTON, indeed, forms a sweeping exception to this rule; but he almost confirms it.

Many of the tales of Chaucer, which are paraphrastical translations from the Latin and Italian languages, prove him to have been a linguist of no ordinary standard; and his prose essays stamp him a logician. It has been already shown that he was well versed in the science of astronomy—as much of it at least as was known in that age. That he was a philosopher in the most practical acceptation of the term—that of humanizing his fellow-creatures, and making them happier as well as wiser, we need only refer to the best and most carefully written of his poems.

As a poet, his chief power lay in description, and this was marvellous; whatever object it is his purpose to delineate, he inspects, and probes, and twists, and turns it on every side, as a botanist pores into a flower; and then he presents it to you clothed in the minute perfection of a Dutch painting with the charms of ease, grace, and freedom superadded. So patiently did he study the characters of the people he described, that he seems not to have more closely examined their costumes, (accurately as he did this,) than he did their habits of thought. Hence, the speeches he puts into their mouths are so truly in keeping, that their great merit almost becomes neutralized in the mind; for we feel that he merely put down what he heard as well as what he saw when describing his characters. The first remark made to us by one who had read for the first time his Prologue to the Canterbury Pilgrims, was, that 'it detracted materially from Mr. Stothard's fame in illustrating it, for that all was there, ready fashioned to his hands.' In this very prologue the portrait of the shipman is a striking likeness to this day. His action on horseback is not yet more accomplished; he still makes progress, as Butler humorously describes him, as though he were 'rowing the horse.' The doctor of physic 'reading little in his bible;' playing into the apothecary's hands; regulating his diet, and eating that which is most nutritious. The showy wife of Bath, so trim about the ankles, with her new tight shoes, and stockings gartered up without a wrinkle. The reeve, (or steward,) contriving to lay his lord under obligations by advancing him money in his necessitous extravagance. The serjeant at law, than whom no man was more busy, 'and yet he seemed busier than he was;' are all as truly pourtrayed as the reflections in a camera lucida. Chaucer is one of the most matter-of-fact poets that ever existed. He describes and recapitulates, and describes and repeats, like one who having beheld a wonder for the first time, returns at every given opportunity to the object of his admiration. He is sometimes tedious in his descriptions; and this appears to arise from an anxiety on his own part, lest the reader should not be able to keep pace with him in feeling at once the full impression of the object he is delineating. The late Mr. Hazlitt, in his lectures on the poets, has most happily in one pithy sentence (a remarkable feature in his critical analyses) struck out

Chaucer's poetical faculty. He says: 'His poetry reads like history. Every thing has a downright reality; at least in the narrator's mind. A simile, or a sentiment, is as if *it were given in upon evidence.*' Again: 'He speaks of what he wishes to describe with the accuracy, the discrimination of one who relates what has happened to himself, or has had the best information from those who have been eye-witnesses of it. The strokes of his pencil always tell. He dwells only on the essential, on that which would be interesting to the persons really concerned: yet as he never omits any material circumstance, he is prolix from the number of points on which he touches, without being diffuse on any one; and is sometimes tedious from the fidelity with which he adheres to his subject, as other writers are from the frequency of their digressions from it. The chain of his history is composed of a number of fine links, closely connected together, and riveted by a single blow.'

* * * * * *

'He is contented to find grace and beauty

in truth. He exhibits for the most part the naked object, with little drapery thrown over it. His metaphors, which are few, are not for ornament, but use, and as like as possible to the things themselves. He does not affect to show his power over the reader's mind, but the power which the subject has over his own.'

* * * * * *

'There is no artificial pompous display, but a strict parsimony of the poet's materials, like the rude simplicity of the age in which he lived.'

It has already been observed that Chaucer was prone to be tedious in his descriptions. In his rural walks he is just as tedious as a sauntering companion by a wood-side, who is a devoted admirer of nature. He who would be impatient with the one for pausing at every furlong to remark and admire the shifting effects of light in the morning clouds; or to hearken to the whistle of the early birds; or to notice the varieties of foliage, the smell of wild blossoms, the juicy freshness and vivid hue of tall plants that bow in graceful homage over the 'huddling brook'—such a one may easily be wearied with the description of the other, for it is commonly an accurate journal of his whole route.

The extraordinary fidelity of his portraits, and the careful minuteness with which he lays on tint after tint to heighten their effect, has already been insisted. This in the main is true; yet will he at times, with one dash of his pencil, (like a true genius,) give all the expression you can require. To take two or three specimens at random, by way of example.— The appearance of Troilus striding across the hall after his return from Cressida, when she was taken from him and delivered up to the Greeks :—

> 'To Troy is come this woful Troilus,
> In sorrow, above all sorrow's smart,
> With *felon-look*, and with face despiteous;
> Then suddenly down from his horse he start,
> And thro' his palace, with a swollen heart,
> To chamber went.'

The love-worn Arcite, who, from the weakness of his spirits, burst into tears if he 'heard song or instrument about the house.' Shakspeare himself could not have surpassed this for the intensity of its truth.

To take a humourous picture, yet no less vivid: the Pardoner, describing himself preaching, says,

> 'Then pain I me to stretchen forth my neck,
> And east and west upon the people I beck,
> As doth a dove sitting upon a barn.'

Here is the full length of a friar in one line:—

> 'Fat as a whale, and *walkèd as a swan*.'

Chanticleer, the herald of the dawn, is thus shortly, yet sufficiently described:—

> 'But when the cock, common astrologer,
> 'Gan on its breast to beat, and after crow.'

It were an easy, and a pleasant task too, to go on multiplying examples of this great poet's accurate eye in description; after that, as many more might be cited of his humour, and keen satire; and a moderate volume would scarcely contain all the strokes of passion and tenderness with which his poems abound. The story of Troilus and Cressida alone, for profound feeling, would honour any poet that ever breathed. Every scene—where the lovers themselves are concerned—is redolent with sighs of 'such sweet breath' as the following. Cressida is absent from her lover, but has promised to return to him in a month:—

> 'And every night, as was his wont to do,
> He stood, the bright moon shining to behold,
> And all his sorrow to the moon he told,
> And said—" Surely when thou art horned new
> I shall be glad—if ALL THE WORLD be true."'

How beautiful the thought! to make his love the whole world, and the whole world to be absorbed in the one idea of his love.

It is needless to say that the above hasty references (single stones exhibited for samples of the complete magnificent structure) have not been addressed to the intimate acquaintance of Chaucer: the design of the present little volume will be considered by such readers; and therefore that they are quoted for the sole purpose of inducing the young and the tasteful, to whom his poems are as yet 'a sealed book,' to prepare themselves for many an hour of delight and wonder. The obsolete dialect and antiquated spelling will for a time be sore stumbling blocks to their progress;—but these overcome, great will be their reward.

The Procession of the Pilgrims to Canterbury.

PROLOGUE,

OR

INTRODUCTION

TO THE

CANTERBURY TALES.

In that pleasant season of the year when the April showers and the soft west wind make the grass and flowers to spring up in every mead and heath, and birds welcome the shining days, it is the custom with people from all parts of the country to set forth on pilgrimages to foreign lands, and more especially to pay their vows at the shrine raised in Canterbury to the holy martyr St. Thomas à Becket.

At this time of the year, I, GEOFFRY CHAUCER, the writer of these Tales, was remaining at the sign of the Tabard, in Southwark, ready to set forth on my pilgrimage to Canterbury. In the evening a company of about nine and twenty persons, bound on the same errand, had assembled in the inn; with all of whom I had made acquaintance before sun-set, and had agreed to journey in their company the following day. Before I enter upon my tale, the reader may desire to know what were the character, condition, and exterior accomplishments of my fellow travellers. These, as they appeared to me, I supply as follows.

The first in order was a worthy KNIGHT, a worshipper from his youth of chivalrous and all gallant deeds; a lover of truth and honour, frankness and courtesy. He had served with renown in his Lord's wars against the Heathen, the Russian, and the Turk; had fought in fifteen battles, and in three tilting matches had slain his foe. With all these rough and unchamber-like accomplishments, he was in his demeanour and address as meek as a young maiden. No villainous or injurious speech was ever heard to pass his lips—in short, he was a perfect knight of gentle blood. As regards his furniture and equipment, he rode a good and serviceable horse, which had become staid, and somewhat the worse from hard campaigning. His dress was a short fustian cassock, or gaberdine, soiled and fretted with his armour; for he had newly arrived from foreign travel, and was proceeding straight to the shrine of our holy martyr at Canterbury.

He was accompanied by his son, a youth about twenty years of age, who acted as his SQUIRE. The person of this young man was tall and well-proportioned, of great strength and activity. Being a bachelor and a lover, he was delicately attentive to his external appearance. His hair, which flowed in rich and natural curls upon his shoulders, was carefully disposed. Hoping to win his lady's favour, he had behaved with bravery in three several expeditions—in Flanders, in Artois, and in Picardy. His gown, which was short, with long open sleeves, was as fresh and gay as a spring meadow embroidered with flowers. Singing and piping all day long, he was as cheerful as the month of May. In addition to all these graces, he was a fine horseman, a tasteful writer of songs, excelled in the tournament and the dance, could write and draw with ease and elegance; and, what is esteemed a principal accomplishment in a squire of high degree, he was worthy to carve at table before his father. Courteous, humble, and dutiful was this fair young man; and withal so devoted to his ladylove, that he would outwatch the doting nightingale.

One other attendant, and no more, had our Knight upon the present occasion; a YEOMAN, dressed in a green coat and hood. He had a head like a nut,[1] and a face of the same colour. In his hand he carried a sturdy bow, and at his side under his belt a sheaf of bright sharp arrows, winged with peacock feathers. His arm was defended by a bracer;[2] on one side hung

---

[1] In the original, it is *not-hed*. This may mean either a 'head like a nut,' as Tyrwhitt has interpreted it, and which seems appropriate to the character of the man described; or *knotte-hed*, a name given to the knob at the end of a staff, and which term still survives in the north of England.

[2] A defence for the arm. '*A bracer*,' says Ascham, 'serves two purposes; one, to save the arrow from the string when loosed upon it, and the coat from creasing; and the other, that the string, gliding sharply and quickly off the bracer, may make a sharper shoot.'—He also adds, 'in a bracer three

a sword and buckler, and on the other a well-appointed dagger, keen as a spear. At his breast hung a silver ornament, also a horn, the girdle or baldrick of which was green. He was a thorough forester, and skilful in all manner of wood-craft.

There was also in our company a Nun, a PRIORESS, called Madam Eglantine, a demure and simply-smiling lady, whose sharpest speech was,—'By Saint Eloi!' She could chaunt by heart the whole of the divine service, sweetly twanging it through her nose. She was mistress of the French language, as it is spoken at the school of Stratford-le-Bow; but the French of Paris was to her unknown. Her conduct at meals was precisely well-bred and delicate, all her anxiety being to display a courteous and stately deportment, and to be regarded in return with esteem and reverence. So charitable and piteous was her nature, that a dead or bleeding mouse in a trap would wring her heart. She kept several little dogs, which

things should be particularly attended to; that it should have no nails in it, no buckles, and that it should be fastened on with laces without tags.'—*Archer's Guide*, 1833, p. 136.

were pampered with roast meat, milk, and the finest bread. Bitterly would she take on, if one were ill-used or dead. In short, she was all conscience and tender heart.

To speak of her features: her nose was long but well-shaped; her eyes light, and grey as glass; her mouth delicately small, soft and red, and her forehead fair and broad. For dress she wore a neatly-made cloak, and a carefully-crimped neckerchief; on her arm was a pair of beads of small coral, garnished with green, from which depended a handsome gold brooch, with a great A engraved upon it, and underneath, the motto, '*Amor vincit omnia.*' (Love overcomes all things.)

In her train was another NUN, who acted as her chaplain; also three Priests.

The next in succession was a MONK, one well calculated to rule his order. He was a bold rider, and fond of hunting. A manly man, and worthy to have been an abbot. Many a capital horse had he in stall: and as he rode along, one could hear his bridle gingling in the whistling wind like the distant chapel bells.[1]

---

[1] It was the fashion in those days to hang bells to the

Our Monk set but little store by the strict regulations of the good old saints; holding rather with modern opinions. For instance, he cared not the value of a straw for that one which denies that a monk can be a hunter and at the same time a holy man; or, that out of his cloister he is like a fish out of water. And, indeed, there is some reason in his objection; for, as he would say, 'Why should he pore all day over his books till his brain is turned, or apply himself to handicraft labour as St. Augustin ordains? Let St. Augustin stick to his day-labour!' For himself, he was a good hard rider outright, and kept his greyhounds, which were as swift as swallows before rain. Coursing was his sole pleasure, and to gratify it he spared no cost.

I noticed that his sleeves were embroidered with the finest grey fur; and his hood fastened under his chin with a curiously chased gold

---

horses' bridles. In the *Faery Queene* the caparison of a lady's steed is thus described:

> 'Her wanton palfrey all was overspred
> With tinsell trappings, woven like a wave,
> Whose *bridle rung with golden bels* and bosses brave.'
>   B. i. Canto ii. Stanza xiii.

F

clasp, at one end of which was wrought a true lover's knot. His head was bald, and shone like glass; his face too seemed as though it had been anointed. His eyes were deeply set, and kept rolling in his head, which glowed and steamed like a furnace. He had any thing but the air of a mortified and *ghostly* father: indeed a roast swan was his favourite dish. A fine and stately horse, as brown as a berry, and boots supple and without a wrinkle, completed the equipment of this choice specimen of a prelate.

There was a FRIAR, a limiter;[1] who, though in appearance a solemn man, was a wanton and merry wag. No man in all the four orders of brotherhood was such an adept in dalliance and smooth speech. Many a young girl had he joined in wedlock free of expense. He was the very prop and stay of his order. He was a favourite with all the country round, and especially cherished by the good dames of the town;—for being a licenciate,[2] he was, by his

---

[1] One licensed to beg alms for his convent, within a certain district.

[2] One licensed by the Pope to hear confessions.

own account, as great in hearing confession as a curate. Sweetly would he dispense the duties of shrift,[1] and pleasant was his absolution. Whenever he expected a handsome pittance, the penance he enjoined was always light; for it is a sign a man has been well shriven when he makes presents to a poor convent.

His tippet was constantly stored with articles of cutlery and knick-knacks, which he distributed among the good wives in his perambulations. To these pleasant qualities, which made him everywhere a welcome guest, he added the grace of being a performer on the lute and a merry singer. In figure he was as well made and strong as a champion of wrestlers; and the skin of his neck was as white as the lady-lily. He was better acquainted with all the taverns, tapsters, and hostlers in the town than with the strolling beggars, the sick, and the miserable: for a man of his worth and calling, it was more convenient as well as befitting, that he should cultivate the acquaintance of the rich, and dispensers of good

---

[1] Confession.

things, than with the diseased and the mendicant. Wherever he spied a chance of profit or advantage there did he direct all his courtesy, and humbly ply his services. He was the expertest beggar in the convent, and obtained a grant that none of the brethren should cross him in his haunts; for if a widow had barely a shoe to her foot, so sweet to her ear was his, 'As it was in the beginning,' &c., that he would extort a farthing from her before his departure. Of him it might be said that 'the labourer was of *more* worth than his hire.' On settling days he was a man of importance, not like a cloisterer, or poor scholar with his threadbare cloak, but rather as master of the order, or even like the Pope himself.

He wore a short cloak of double-woven worsted, round as a lady's dress, uncrushed. He would lisp in his speech from wantonness, or to give effect to his English: and while he was singing, his eyes would twinkle like the stars in a frosty night. The name of this worthy limiter was Hubert.

There was a MERCHANT with a forked beard,

and dressed in a motley suit, with a Flemish beaver hat. His boots were of the best manufacture, neatly clasped. He sat high upon his horse, and delivered his opinions in a solemn tone, always sounding forth the increase of his winnings. He was for having the sea securely guarded, for the benefit of trade, between Middleburgh and Orwell. His skill and knowledge in the various exchanges of money were remarkable; and so prudently did he order his bargains and speculations, that he was esteemed a man of credit and substance.

There was a CLERK, or scholar, of Oxford also, who was deeply skilled in logic. His horse was as lean as a rake, and he himself was not overfed, but looked hollow and staidly sober. His surtout cloak was of the threadbare class; for he had hitherto obtained no living, and not being a man of the world he was unfit for an office. He had rather have at his bed's head twenty books of Aristotle and his philosophy than the costliest wardrobe and furniture. Though a philosopher however, he had not yet discovered the golden secret of science; but all that he could scrape from his friends was forthwith spent in books of learning. Fervently would he pray for the souls of those who would assist him to purchase instruction; for study was the sole care of his life. In conversation he never uttered a word more than was necessary, and that was said with a modest propriety, shortly and quickly, and full of meaning. His discourse was pregnant with morality, and he as gladly afforded as received instruction.

A Sergeant-at-Law, cautious and shrewd, who had been often at consultation, was there also. A prudent and deferential man. He had been frequently appointed justice of assize by patent and commission. Many were the fees and robes with which he had been presented on account of his great legal knowledge and renown. There was no purchaser like him, and his dealings were above suspicion. He was the busiest of men, and yet he seemed more busy than he was. He had at his fingers' ends all the terms, cases, and judgments from the time of the Conquest; and in his indictments, the man was clever that could detect a flaw. He knew all the statutes by heart. He rode in a plain coat of mixed cloth, fastened with a narrow-striped silken girdle.

A country Gentleman, commonly called a FRANKLIN, was in our company. He had a fresh coloured rosy face, and a beard as white as a daisy. A sop in wine was his favourite morning beverage: for he was a true son of Epicurus, believing that the most perfect happiness consisted in perfect enjoyment. He possessed a noble mansion, and was the most hospitable of entertainers. He dined at quality hours—always after one o'clock; and so plenteously stored was his table, that his house may be said to have snowed meat and drink—fish, flesh, and fowl; and of these the daintiest. His suppers were furnished according to the season. Many a fat partridge had he in his preserve; and stewed bream or pike was a common dish at his board. Ill befel his cook if the sauce were too pungent, or his dinner not punctually served. He kept open house, and the dining table in hall remained covered the whole day.

He had been at several times justice of the peace, sheriff, steward of the hundred court, and knight of the shire. Among all the country gentlemen round, there was not his compeer. At his girdle, which was as white as morning milk, hung a dagger and a silken purse.

A HABERDASHER and a CARPENTER, a WEAVER, a DYER, and a worker of TAPESTRY, members of a solemn and large fraternity, were all clothed in the same costume. Their furniture was all spick and span new. Their knives were not of the common description, mounted with brass, but wrought with pure silver. Their girdles and pouches also were equally costly. Each seemed to be of the respectable class of burgesses, who take the uppermost seats [1] in the Guildhall. Their grave and sensible demeanour befitted them for the office of aldermen. They were men of landed estate and wealthy in cattle; and this their wives had no objection to, for it is a fine thing to be styled '*Madam*,' and to walk, with your train supported like a queen, in the first ranks to church.

[1] The raised floor at the end of the hall was called a *dais*.

The company had a Cook with them upon this occasion. He was the man of all others to tell you a draught of London ale out of a hundred. No one could match him in roasting and boiling; his made-dishes, potted beef, raised pies, and blanc-mangers, were absolutely eminent.

There was a Shipman, or merchantman too, a West-countryman; I think he came from Dartmouth: he rode upon a hack—as well as he was able: and wore a gown of coarse stuff, which came down as low as his knee: also a dagger suspended by a lace from his neck under his arm. The hot summer had made his face all brown—he was a fine hearty looking fellow. Many and many a cask of wine had he brought from Bourdeaux while the merchants were fast asleep in their beds. He was not remarkable for tenderness of conscience, seeing that if he were engaged at sea, and had got the upper-hand, he always sent his prisoners home *by water*.[1] But for skill in reckoning his tides; for knowing all the

---

[1] This passage, which in the original appears to be rather

currents, shallows, and sandbanks; the exact place of the sun, the age of the moon, and for the complete art of piloting, there was not his equal between Hull and Carthage. He was a brave, and prudent man; whose beard many a tempest had shaken. He was intimate with every harbour from Gothland to Cape Finisterre, and every creek in Spain and Brittany. His ship was called the Magdalen.

There was a DOCTOR of PHYSIC with us. No one was like him for discoursing on medicine and surgery; for he was well grounded in astronomy. He kept his patients principally by his magic, and could render them fortunate by the ascendant of his images. He was a skilful practitioner, and knew the cause of every malady; whether it were cold, heat, moisture, or drouth; where it originated, and from what humour;—the cause and root of his

obscure, I think is intended to convey a sly little irony;—for the poet, after saying,

'*Of nice conscience toke he no kepe,*'

adds,

'If that he faught and hadde the higher hand,
By *water* he sent hem home to every land.'

In other words I conceive the meaning to be, that he *drowned* his prisoners.

complaint being discovered, he would quickly set the patient on his legs again. His apothecaries were ever at his beck and call, to pour in their drugs and electuaries—for they played into each others' hands. Their friendship was of long standing. He was well read in the old authors Esculapius, Dioscorides, and Rufus; Old Galen, Halius, and Hippocrates, and a host besides. He was very measured and exact in his diet, avoiding superfluity, and always selecting that which was most nourishing and digestible. His Bible he studied but little. His dress was a rose-coloured Persian, lined with thin silk, or taffeta; yet he was but easy in his circumstances. He carefully laid by all his gains during the pestilence; for gold is well known to be a cordial in medicine; gold therefore he held in especial reverence.

A good WIFE OF BATH made one of our company. She was unfortunately rather deaf, and had lost some of her teeth. She carried on a trade in cloth-making, which excelled the manufactures of Ypres and Ghent. No wife in all the parish could take precedence of her at mass; and if one ever so presumed, she was wroth out of all charity. The kerchiefs which adorned her head on Sundays were of the finest web, and I dare swear weighed a pound. Her hose were of a brilliant scarlet, gartered up without a wrinkle; and her shoes tight and new. She had been ever esteemed a worthy woman, and had accompanied to church five husbands in her time. Having thrice travelled to Jerusalem, crossing many a strange river, and having visited Rome, Saint James's,[1] Cologne, with its three kings, and passed through Galicia, she had a world of intelligence to communicate by the way. Her dress consisted of a spruce neckerchief; a hat as broad as a target; a mantle wrapping her fair large hips, and on her feet was a pair of sharp spurs. She rode upon an ambling pony. In company she took her share in the laugh, and would display her remedies for all complaints in love: she could play a good hand at that game.

There was also a religious man; who was a

---

[1] St. James's of Compostella, in Spain.

poor Village Parson: yet was he rich in holy thought and works, as well as in learning—a faithful preacher of the gospel of Christ; full of gentleness and diligence; patient in adversity, and forbearing. So far was he from distressing for his tithes, that he disbursed his offerings, and almost his whole substance among his poor parishioners. A pittance sufficed him. The houses in his parish were situate far asunder, yet neither wind and rain, nor storm and tempest could keep him from his duty; but, with staff in hand, would he visit the remotest, great and small, rich and poor. This noble example he kept before his flock; that first he himself performed, what he afterwards preached, joining this figure with his admonition: 'If gold will rust, what will not iron do?' For, if a priest in whom we confide become tarnished, a wonder if the frail layman keep himself unpolluted. The priest should set an example of purity to his flock; for how shameful a sight is a foul shepherd and cleanly sheep!

He did not let out his benefice to hire, and desert his flock to run up to London for the purpose of seeking promotion; but steadily kept home, and guarded well the fold. He was the true shepherd, and no hireling. Moreover, holy and virtuous as he was, he turned an eye of pity upon the sinful man, mingling his lecture with discretion and benignity. It was the business of his life, by good example, to lead his fellow creatures gently to heaven. The obstinate and stiff necked, however, whether in high or low estate, were sure to receive from him a severe rebuke. A better priest I know not, far or near. He craved neither pomp nor reverence, or betrayed any affected scrupulousness of conscience: but the doctrine of Christ and his apostles he taught with simplicity, first following it himself.

He had a brother with him—a PLOUGHMAN, who had in his time scattered many a load of dung: a thorough hard labourer, living in peace and perfect charity with all men. Above all things, and at all times, he best loved his God and Creator, and then his neighbour as himself. When it lay in his power he would finish a job of threshing for a poor man without hire. He paid his tithes fairly and punctually, both of his produce and live stock. He was dressed in a tabard,[1] and rode upon a mare. There were also a REEVE,[2] and a MILLER; a SUMMONER,[3] a PARDONER,[4] a MANCIPLE,[5] and myself.

The MILLER was a hardy churl, brawny and large of bone. He always bore away the prize ram in wrestling matches. He was short shouldered, broad and stubby. Massive indeed was the door that he could not heave from its hinges, or crack with the butting of his head. His beard was sandy, like a fox or a sow, and cut broad and square in the shape of spade. He had a wart on his nose, adorned with a tuft, red as the bristles of a hog's ear. His nostrils were wide and black; and mouth

---

[1] A jacket without sleeves; worn in the first instance by noblemen in the wars: in later times, by heralds, and was their coat of arms in service. From Chaucer's having clad the *ploughman* in such a garment, he probably meant to convey the hint that it was a cast-off dress.

[2] A steward or bailiff.

[3] An officer employed to summon delinquents to appear in the ecclesiastical courts; now called an *apparitor*.

[4] A seller of pardons or indulgences from the Pope.

[5] An officer who has the care of purchasing victuals for an inn of court. The office still subsists in several colleges as well as inns of court.

gaped like a furnace. He was a roaring roystering madcap; who upon occasion would try the strength of his conscience by filching his customers' corn, and giving them false tales.[1] Yet, withal, he had 'a thumb of gold,' as the old saying goes respecting honest millers; and I believe was no worse than his brethren. He wore a white coat with a blue hood, and a sword and buckler at his side. He was a performer on the bagpipe, and with it marshalled us out of town.

There was a gentle MANCIPLE, who was a pattern to all caterers and purchasers of provision; for whether he paid in ready money or went upon credit, he always so managed his accounts as to have a surplus of cash in hand. Now, this appears to me like a special gift from heaven, that an ignorant man of this stamp should be able to outwit a whole bevy of learned clerks. He had more than thirty masters, acute in the law, a dozen of whom were fit to be stewards to any nobleman in the

---

[1] The old term for reckoning, is a '*tale*.'
'And every shepherd tells his *tale*,
Under the hawthorn in the dale.'
Milton's *Allegro*.

land, and keep his estate free from debt and incumbrance (if he had the brains to let them) or assist him to live as frugally as he might desire; and even to order and arrange the public affairs of a county:—yet was this manciple a match for them all.

The REEVE was a slender choleric man; his beard was close shaven like stubble; and hair cropped round his ears, with a forelock like a priest. His legs were long and straight as a pike, without a hint of calf. He was an excellent manager of a granary, and no auditor could catch him tripping in his accounts. He could give a shrewd guess what would be the produce of the land after rain or drouth. He had been bailiff to his lord from the year of his coming of age; consequently had the care and accounting of his whole stock. He was alive to all the tricks and contrivances of the labourers and other bailiffs, so that they stood in awe of him as they would of death himself. He had a handsome house upon a heath 'bosomed high' in green trees: and, in short, was better provided than his master; for he had secretly amassed considerable property, which he would upon occasion artfully lend to his lord in his necessities, and thus confer an easy obligation out of his own superfluity. In his youth he had learned a handicraft, and was a good carpenter and wheelwright. Our Reeve rode a well-conditioned dapple-grey stallion, that he used to call Scot. He wore a long surtout of light blue, and a rusty sword at his side. I heard that the town of Baldswell in Norfolk was his birthplace. His dress was tucked up all round like a friar's, and he always kept in the rear of our company.

There was a SUMMONER with us, whose face was like one of the fiery cherubim; for it was studded with red hot carbuncles. He had small puckered eyes, scurfy brows, and a black scanty beard. The children were frightened at the sight of him. No lotion or ointment could rid his cheeks of those filthy knobs and excrescences. His favourite food and beverage were garlic, leeks, and onions, and the strongest bodied red wine: then would he shout and rave like a madman, speaking nothing but Latin—he had caught up a few terms out of some law decree; and no wonder, for he heard nothing else all day; and everyone knows that a jay can speak what he has been taught, as well as the Pope himself; but let anyone try him a little farther, and he would find his philosophy quite spent. '*Questio quid juris?*' would then be his answer. He was, however, a kind fellow in his way, and would, for a quart of wine or so, wink at his neighbours' delinquencies. But if he found one with a good warm purse, he would tell him he need not care for the Archdeacon's malediction just as if a man's soul were in his purse; for in purse he should be punished. 'The purse,' would he say, 'is the Archdeacon's hell:' in all which I pronounce him to be an *arch* deceiver; since the guilty man should ever stand in awe of a curse, which will destroy the soul, as absolution will preserve it. Of the 'significavit'[1] also, let him beware.

He contrived to make himself acquainted with all the cabals and little arrangements of the young folks in the diocese, and kept them upon their good behaviour. He had sur-

---

[1] The beginning of the sentence of excommunication.

mounted that extraordinary head of his with a garland large enough for an alehouse sign at a fair: a spacious cake also seemed to serve the two purposes of buckler and provender.

A gentle PARDONER rode also with this wight —his friend and compeer. He was originally from Ronceveaux, and had now newly arrived from the Court of Rome. The burthen of the song, 'Come hither, love, to me,' was constantly running in his head, which he shouted at the full stretch of his lungs; the Summoner all the while accompanying him with a stiff bass, as if it had been a double clarion. This Pardoner had smooth yellow hair, which hung by ounces about him, like a strike of flax, overspreading his shoulders. In the gaiety of his heart he wore no hood, but kept it packed up in his wallet; so he rode with his head bare, save and except a cap, in which was fastened a vernicle.[1] He prided himself upon

---

[1] A picture of Jesus Christ in miniature. It was usual with persons returning from pilgrimages to bring with them certain tokens of the several places which they had visited. The Pardoner, therefore, had this vernicle in his cap in token of his visit to Rome, where in the church of St. Peter was preserved the miniature in question, miraculously imprinted upon a handkerchief.

his sitting on horseback, as being after the newest fashion. Before him lay his wallet stuffed with pardons, all hot from Rome. He had a full glaring eye, like a hare's; a sneaking voice like a goat's; and a chin which never owned the inheritance of a beard.

And now to speak of his profession. If you were to search from Ware to Berwick-upon-Tweed, you would not meet with such another Pardoner. Among his relics he could produce a pillow-covering, which he pronounced to be the Virgin Mary's veil; a small piece of the seal which St. Peter had with him when he walked upon the sea; a brazen cross set with brilliants; and some pig's bones in a glass. With these relics he would make in one day more money among the poor country people than the parson would in two months. Thus with his flattery and his falsities he made fools of both priest and people.

Notwithstanding all this, however, I must acknowledge that he was a famous churchman. He read the service with dignity and emphasis; though he shone to greater advantage at the

Offertory;[1] for he knew that the sermon would then succeed, in which it behoved him to polish up his tongue for the purpose of procuring a handsome collection afterwards, wherein he was successful. Therefore, in the anticipation of it, he would sing like a blackbird after rain.

Thus have I related to you briefly the list, the calling, the array, and the purport of that assembly's being collected at the above-mentioned inn in Southwark, called the Tabard, adjoining the Bell. And now it behoves me to inform you of certain arrangements we made that night; after which I shall proceed to describe our journey, and the remainder of our pilgrimage.

In the first place, however, let me here apologise for any improprieties I may hereafter commit in relating each man's tale; since it is my design to rehearse them as nearly as I can recollect, according to the style and manner in which they were delivered by the narrator.

---

[1] That portion of the Roman Catholic service which immediately precedes the blessing of the bread and wine. It is always sung.

Our host set before us at supper an excellent entertainment; the food and the wine were of the best quality. He was a comely man, large in person, with sunken eyes, and worthy to have been created marshal in a hall. The whole ward of Cheap cannot boast a fairer citizen. Bold and manly, plain and sensible in speech, at the same time merry withal, he thus addressed the company after we had all paid our reckonings. 'Now, my masters, permit me to welcome you heartily to your inn; for, by my truth I have not this year seen so honourable a company as is now assembled beneath this roof. Fain would I contribute to your amusement were it in my power. In proof of which a thought has just struck me, which will cost you nothing. You are all about to journey to Canterbury—God and the blessed martyr reward you!—Well,—as you travel along, you will be for whiling the way with gossip and glee: for truly there is little comfort in journeying as dumb as a stone. If, therefore, you will abide by my judgment, and proceed to-morrow as I shall direct, by the spirit of my father which is in heaven, whip off my head if I do not make you a merry company. Without more ado, hold up your hands if you agree to my proposal.'

Our consent was not long to seek, seeing that there was no occasion for much deliberation; we therefore granted him his terms, and bade him speak on.

'To come to the point then, my masters: each of you on his way to and from Canterbury shall relate two adventures, and whoso shall acquit himself the best,—that is, in tales of most mirth and judgment, shall have a supper here at the general expense, upon your return from Canterbury. And to contribute to your entertainment, I will myself ride with you at my own cost, and be your guide. Farthermore, let me make a condition that whoever shall call my judgment in question, he shall bear the whole cost of the journey. If you grant me my conditions, say so at once, and I will early prepare for my undertaking.'

We cheerfully bound ourselves to abide by his terms, at the same time engaging him to be our governor, to sit in judgment upon the merits of our stories, also to provide our supper at a stated price per head; and that we would —both high and low—be ruled by his decision. All this, and the wine at the same time, having been discussed, without longer delay, we all went to roost.

At day-spring up rose our host, and was chanticleer to the whole company, collecting us together in a flock; and forth we rode at a walking pace to the watering-place of St. Thomas; when he drew up his horse and said: 'My masters, you bear in mind your covenant. —Now let us see who shall tell the first tale; and so sure as I drink ale or wine, whoever shall rebel against my judgment, shall pay all the costs of the journey. Before we proceed farther, draw lots, and let him who draws the shortest, begin.'

'Sir Knight,' said he, 'my lord and master, be pleased to draw: and come you near, my Lady Prioress: and you, Sir Clerk, oblige us by laying aside your bashfulness and your studying: so—every man lay hand.'

After each had drawn, the lot fell upon the Knight, to the satisfaction of the whole company.

When this worthy man found he must abide by the general covenant, he said:—'Since I am fated to begin this sport, in Heaven's name welcome be the lot. Let us ride on, and listen to my tale.'

With cheerful countenance he then began, and said as you shall hear.

THE KNIGHT'S TALE:

THE STORY OF PALAMON AND ARCITE.

In former days there lived a warrior named Theseus; he was King of Athens, and in his time had been so famous in deeds of arms, that he was the most renowned under the sun. He had conquered many a wealthy kingdom, and by his skill and knightly conduct had subdued the whole territory of the Amazons, which formerly was called Scythia. He married the young queen of that country (her name was Ippolita), and brought her and her young sister, Emily, home with him to Athens in great pomp and solemnity. And thus accompanied by song and triumph I leave this valiant king, riding into Athens, surrounded by his host in arms.

And here, if it were not tedious to relate, I would describe to you fully the manner in which Theseus overcame the kingdom of the Amazons; also the great battle between the Amazons and the Athenians; how Ippolita, the fair and valiant Queen of Scythia, was besieged; of the feast that was held at her wedding; and of the temple that was raised upon her coming home to Athens: but I have other matter in hand, for my story will be found long enough; and as I would not willingly prevent every man in turn from telling his tale, I will continue mine, and let us see who shall win the supper.

This King of whom I made mention, riding along in his pride and prosperity, as he approached near to Athens, perceived kneeling in the highway a company of ladies, by two and two, clad all in black, who made so doleful a weeping and lamentation as the like was never heard: neither would they cease till they had laid hands upon his horse's bridle and stopped his procession.

'What people are ye,' said Theseus, 'who at my return home thus interrupt my festival with your grievous weeping? Are you envious of my honour and success, that you thus wail and lament? or hath any one offended you? Let me know, if your wrong can be repaired: likewise the reason of your being clad in this woful black.'

The eldest lady of the party, whom it was ruth and pity to see and hear, then spake: 'We do not grieve, my lord, at the success of your victory, your glory, and your honour; but we beseech of your mercy help and succour: have compassion upon our woe and our distress! In thy gentle nature let fall one drop of pity upon us wretched women; for of a truth, my lord, there is not one of us all but she has been either a Duchess or a Queen; now, thanks to the falsehood of fortune, with whom no lot is steadfast, we are both miserable and desolate. For fifteen days past have we waited your home-coming, here in the temple of the Goddess Clemency: let not our errand fail, but aid us since you have the power.

'I, miserable creature, was formerly wife to King Capaneus who perished at Thebes; and all we who thus lament, lost our husbands during the siege of that place: and yet old Creon, who, alas! is now King of Thebes, in his wrath and wickedness, has wreaked his spite and tyranny on the dead bodies of our lords, which he ordered to be drawn together in a heap, and with no entreaty will allow them to be burned or buried, but has left them a prey to the wild dogs.' And with that speech, they grovelled on the ground piteously weeping.

When this gentle conqueror heard them so speak, his heart ached to think that those who were then before him in such a plight had been persons of high estate; so, leaping from his horse, he went and raised them from the ground, bidding them be comforted, for that upon the oath of a true knight he would so avenge them upon the tyrant Creon, that all Greece should acknowledge the deserved death he would receive from the hand of Theseus.

Whereupon, without delay, or even entering Athens, he raised his banner, and with his host rode forth towards Thebes; the Queen, Ippolita, and her young sister, the lovely Emily, he left in Athens awaiting his return. His broad white banner, embroidered in red with the figure of the God Mars, and his ensign, rich in gold tissue, embossed with that of the Minotaur, slain by him in Crete, went glittering through the distant plains. So rode this valiant chief, the flower of chivalry, till he arrived before the walls of Thebes. To shorten this part of my story, he fought with Creon hand to hand, slew him in fair battle, and routed his forces. Afterwards he carried the city by assault, rased its walls, and finally restored to the ladies the remains of their murdered husbands, that they might inter them with the customary rites and solemnity. I pass over the account of the dirge and lament made by those ladies at the funeral pyre, as well as the knightly conduct observed towards them by the noble Theseus when they took their departure.

After the fight, Theseus remained all night upon the field of battle, and disposed of the conquered territory in vassalage according to his pleasure. At the same time the plunderers busied themselves in ransacking the bodies of the slain, stripping them of their armour and clothes. It so happened that in one heap they found, grievously wounded, two young knights lying side by side, both dressed in the same armour, which was richly wrought. Palamon was the name of one knight, and Arcite that of the other. The heralds recognised them as members of the royal family of Thebes; they were sons of two sisters. The plunderers drew them forth from the heaps of the slain, and bore them tenderly to the tent of Theseus, who soon had them conveyed to Athens, and strictly confined in prison, rejecting every offer that was proposed for their ransom. The campaign being over, the king returned home with his army, crowned with the conqueror's laurels, and in joy and honour passed the remainder of his days. But in sorrow and anguish poor Palamon and Arcite were kept close prisoners in a tower, without hope of redemption; the power of gold was unavailing.

Thus passed day after day—year after year; till, one **May** morning, it happened that Emily, who was more beautiful to behold than the lily upon its tall and slender stalk of green, and fresher than the young flowers in May, (for her complexion rivalled the blushing wild-rose) had arisen according to her custom at break of day to do honour to that sweet season of the year; for the slothful and ungentle heart claims no kindred with the lovely May. Her dress was elegant and precise; and her golden hair, braided in tresses, flowed down her back. As the sun was climbing the heavens, she walked up and down the garden, gathering the many-coloured flowers to weave into a garland for her head; and like an angel she sang in the clear air of morning. The thick and strong walls of the tower, which formed the dungeon-keep to the castle, that confined these knights, adjoined the garden in which Emily was taking her pleasure.

In that bright sun and clear morning, Palamon, the woful prisoner, had, as was his custom, with the permission of his gaoler, been taking his walk in an upper chamber of the castle, from whence he had a view of all the noble city, and could look immediately

H

down upon the garden and all its fresh verdure.

The melancholy captive pacing his chamber to and fro, bitterly regretting his fate, by chance caught a sight of Emily through the massy bars of his chamber window, and suddenly started as though stung to the heart. This roused the attention of Arcite, who thinking that he was affected by some recollection of his former fortune, tenderly enquired why he had turned so pale. 'My beloved cousin,' said he, 'for the love of heaven, take in patience our confinement;—it cannot be helped; fortune has laid this adversity upon us, and we must endure it with constancy.'

Palamon replied, 'My dear cousin, you are mistaken in the cause of my grief: the bitter restraint of this prison has not wounded me upon the present occasion, but the beauty of a lady whom I see yonder walking in the garden has so stricken my heart, that it will in all likelihood prove my bane. Whether she be woman or goddess, I know not; but if, O Venus,' said he, (and then he sank passionately on his knees,) 'it hath been thy will to be thus transfigured before me, a wretched and sorrowful creature, assist our escape from this prison: but if the eternal word of fate has doomed us here to die, have compassion upon our kindred, brought so low by oppression and tyranny.'

At this moment Arcite also perceived the lady, and was as much affected as Palamon, and even more, by her surpassing beauty. 'If,' said he, 'I may not be granted the blessing of even looking upon her again, my doom is fixed.'

When Palamon heard these words he turned upon him fiercely, and answered, ' Is this said in soberness or in jest?'

'Seriously by my truth,' said Arcite, ' or evil befall me.'

'Then,' replied Palamon, knitting his brows, ' it were no great honour to you to be false, and a traitor to me, your cousin and brother, who have so deeply sworn to each other, that nothing but death should separate us, and dissolve the pledge: that neither in love nor in any event we should cross each other; but that upon all occasions you should as faithfully serve me, as I should forward your good fortune.

This was our oath, and which you dare not gainsay. You are of my counsel, and yet falsely would presume to love the lady whom I love, and ever shall so long as I live. Truly, therefore, Arcite, I first loved her, and made you, my sworn brother, my confidant: as a true knight, then, are you bound to assist me according to the extent of your power; or else I dare to pronounce you false to your honour.'

Arcite haughtily retorted upon him, that *he* was the false one: 'And false you are,' said he; 'I tell you utterly false. I first loved her. What! you, who even now could not say whether she were a woman or a goddess! Yours is a holy affection, mine for an earthly creature; and I therefore disclosed to you my mind, as to my cousin and sworn brother. Grant it even, that you first loved her, have you forgotten that saying of the old writer— " Who shall give laws to a lover? Love is itself a higher law than any framed by man!" All decrees, therefore, however stern, are daily broken in favour of the more positive commands of love. Whether maiden or widow, a man must needs love in spite of his head; he cannot help himself. There is no likelihood that you, any more than myself, shall ever stand in her favour; seeing that we are condemned to perpetual imprisonment without hope of ransom. We are but like the two hounds striving for a bone; which, when they were spent with rage, a kite bore away from both. At the King's Court, therefore, my brother, "each man for himself," say I: love, if you are inclined; for I love, and ever shall. Here in this prison must we remain, and take what may befall us.'

Great was the strife between them, which lasted longer than I have leisure to tell:—but to my story. It happened one day, that a worthy king, named Perithous, who had been the companion of Theseus from their childhood, came to Athens upon a visit to his friend: for so great was the affection between them, that, according to the old tradition, when one died, the other went down into Tartarus to seek him there. But this is beside my tale.

King Perithous entertained a strong regard for Arcite, and had known him some years in Thebes. At the earnest entreaty, therefore, of Perithous, Theseus granted the young prisoner his liberty without ransom, to go wherever he pleased, with this express provision, that if he ever after were discovered for one moment, by day or by night, within any district of the territory belonging to Theseus, that he should lose his head without redemption.

Now were the perplexity and sorrow of Arcite at their height. Release from affliction had now become his bane: 'Had I never known Perithous,' said he, ' I might still have been dwelling with Theseus, though fettered in his prison : I had then been in bliss ; for the simple sight of her whom I serve, although I might never have merited the favour of her regard, would have been sufficient recompence to me. Yours is the victory, my dear Palamon, in this adventure : for you will remain in this blessed prison :—prison did I call it ?—a paradise. And now, since fortune has been so adverse to me, that I am to endure the absence from her, while you enjoy her sight, the possibility is, that being an honourable and valiant knight, you may hereafter by some farther favour of fortune, be placed in the full attainment of all you desire, while I am exiled, and barren of her sweet favour. Farewell, dear lady! my life, my comfort, my gladness!'

Palamon, on the other hand, when he found his companion in durance gone from him—his cousin, brother, counsellor, and friend—grievously lamented his own fate, and made the great tower resound with lamentation: the very fetters on his legs were wet with bitter tears. 'Alas!' said he, 'Arcite, heaven knows that you are now reaping the fruit of our contention. You are now wandering at large in your native Thebes, little heeding my distress. You may, in your wisdom and manhood, assemble all our kindred, and make so fierce an attack upon this country, that either by chance or treaty, you may be able to win my lady to wife. For, since you are now from bondage free, and a lord again, all the advantage is yours; while I am pining away in captivity.

With this the fire of jealousy burst forth, and so maddened his brain, that his hue became pale as dead ashes: and he cried aloud, 'O ye implacable gods! that govern this world by the bond of your eternal word, and whose will and ordinances are graven on tables of adamant, what more in your sight are the race of mankind than sheep huddled in the fold? For, like another beast, man is slain; and pounded in prison, and tormented: he suffers sickness, and great adversity, and often with a guiltless and unupbraiding heart.' Many such impatient complaints did he continue to pour forth; but I must leave him for a time, and give you some tidings of Arcite.

The summer had passed away, and the long nights increased the distresses both of the lover and the prisoner. It were hard to say whose condition was the more deplorable. Palamon condemned to perpetual imprisonment, loaded with chains and fetters: Arcite exiled evermore from the country where his lady dwelt, and never again to behold her face. I would put the question to you, who are lovers, which of these two had the harder lot; the one who is able to see his lady day by day, yet must ever remain in prison; or the other, who can go whither he pleases, but must never again look upon her whom he loves?

When Arcite returned to Thebes, his loss so pressed upon his heart that he became estranged from sleep and food: he grew lean and hollow-eyed; and his complexion was sallow and pale as ashes. Comfortless and desolate, he always remained alone; and if he happened to hear a song or instrument he would weep without avail, so feeble were his spirits, and he altogether so changed, that his voice was strange to those who knew him.

After enduring for some time this distraction, he one night, in sleep, thought that the winged Mercury stood before him, and bid him be of good cheer. The god was arrayed as when he closed the eyes of Argus; his sleep-compelling wand he held upright before him, and upon his shining locks he wore a winged cap. 'To Athens,' said he, 'shall you go; there will you see an end to all your grief.'

With that word Arcite started and awoke. 'Whatever ill befall me,' said he, 'to Athens *will* I go: no dread of death shall prevent my seeing the lady whom I love and serve: in her presence I care not to die.' Then observing how much he was changed, both in appearance and colour, he thought that if he bore himself in lowly condition, he might live unknown in

Athens, and thus behold his lady almost every day. With this he changed his suit for that of a poor labourer; and all alone, except with one attendant, who knew his secret and all his fortune, and was disguised as poorly as himself, to Athens he travelled straightway. One day he went to Court, and at the gate proffered his services to do such menial work as might be required. To cut the matter short, he fell in with the chamberlain to the Lady Emily, who hired him to hew wood and draw water, being young and large of bone.

Having served a year or two as page of the chamber to the fair Emily, under the name of Philostrate, he so wrought upon all who knew him at the Court, by the gentleness of his condition, that all said it would be advisable for Theseus to raise him in his degree, and give him honourable service, in which he might prove his quality. And thus so enhanced was the fame of his conduct and fair speech, that Theseus promoted him to be near his person, and appointed him squire of his chamber; at the same time giving him gold to maintain his dignity. He also secretly received his rent from his own country, but he used it honourably and with such discretion, that no man wondered how he had it. Three years he passed in this manner, and so conducted himself both in peace and war, that Theseus prized no one more dearly than him. Having brought Arcite to this state of happiness, I will now return awhile to Palamon.

In a strong prison, and in horrible gloom, Palamon had sat for seven long years, wasting with love and sorrow. In the seventh year, however, during a night of May, it happened (whether by chance or destiny) that, through the aid of a friend, he broke from prison soon after midnight. He had so plied his gaoler with wine, drugged with narcotics, that he slept like death; and thus he was enabled to escape.

The night being short, and the day near at hand, he was compelled to lie hidden; his purpose being to remain close all day, and in the night to journey on towards Thebes; where, having arrived, he would rouse his friends to help him war on Theseus, in which attempt he resolved either to die, or win his Lady Emily.

To a grove, then hard by, Palamon stalked with fearful foot.

The lark, the active messenger of day, had welcomed the grey dawn with its song; and the flaming sun had risen, rejoicing the whole heaven, and drying up with his fiery streams the silver drops that hung upon the leaves; when Arcite, who was then, as I have told you, principal squire in the Royal Court of Theseus, arose and looked upon the cheerful day. Ever pondering on the object of his love, he mounted his steed, restless and starting like flame, and rode forth from Court a mile or two, till he came to the grove already mentioned, for the purpose of weaving a garland of woodbine and hawthorn, in honour of the merry month; and all the way he sang a roundelay in the clear sunshine. Having dismounted, he wandered up and down the spot near where Palamon, alarmed lest he should be discovered, lay cowering in a bush. Little was he aware that Arcite was so nigh at hand; and the other was as unmindful as his companion of the close witness to all his words and actions that was there. Well may it be said that fields and woods have eyes and ears.

When Arcite had roamed about to his satisfaction, and finished his May-morning carol, he suddenly lapsed into a thoughtful study. These lovers, in their fantastic moods, are ever wavering. One minute they are swaying and dancing on the tip-top spray of ecstasy; the next, grovelling among the thorns and briars: now up, now down, like a bucket in a well. They are like Friday, which seldom resembles the other days in the week—now rain, now shine. So the Goddess of Love overcasts the hearts of her worshippers, and makes them as variable as the complexion of the day devoted to her worship.[1]

When Arcite had sung his song he began thoughtfully to sigh at the remembrance of his native Thebes, warred on by the revengeful Juno. 'Alas!' said he, 'the royal blood of Cadmus and Amphion is confounded and scattered abroad—Cadmus, the founder of Thebes, and its first crowned King! and here, I, who

---

[1] Friday was devoted to the worship of the Goddess *Venus*. The Romans entitled it 'The day of Venus'—'Dies Veneris.'

am descended from him, and am of the royal stock, am now so thralled a wretch as to be the mere Squire of my mortal enemy, and am moreover compelled to conceal my real name. All my lineage, alas! are gone, with the exception of poor Palamon, whom Theseus keeps a martyr in bondage. And, to crown all my griefs, love for the fair Emily has so possessed my heart, that these would fade away could I but render myself acceptable in her eyes.'

At these words up started Palamon, like one who had suddenly felt a cold sword glide through his heart. With a face pale from rage (as a maniac's) he rushed from the thick brake, and cried: 'Now you are caught, false Arcite! wicked traitor! You, who are of my blood, and my sworn counsellor, still hold your affection for my Lady Emily, that has caused my greatest sorrow. You have deceived King Theseus, and changed your name. Either I or thou shalt die; for no one but myself, while I live, shall love my lady. I, Palamon, your mortal foe, swear this; and though I have no weapon in this place, having newly made my escape from prison, either relinquish the Lady

Emily or die. Choose at once, for there is no escape for you.'

When Arcite had recognised him, and listened to his speech, with a lion's rage he drew his sword, and said, 'By the great Jove, who sitteth above us, were it not that you are mad for love, and are weaponless, you should never quit this grove alive. I deny the pledge and bond which you pretend I made with you. Fool!—again I tell you, love is free; and, in your despite, love her I will. But as you are a worthy Knight, and of gentle[1] blood, and desire to win her by battle, I here give you my word of honour, that to-morrow, without disclosing the affair to any other being, I will not fail to be found here equipped as a Knight, and I will bring accoutrements for you, and you shall select according to your pleasure. Moreover, I will now bring you food and covering for the coming night. If, in this wood, you slay me, and win my lady,

---

[1] The ancient term 'gentle' was used only to imply high breeding. A gentle knight was a knight of high family. In some parts of England, to this day, the best white bread is called 'gentle bread,' to distinguish it from the brown or common.

the prize is your own.' Palamon accepted his challenge, and so they separated until the morrow. Truly is it said that neither love nor royalty can endure fellowship in dominion: and so found Palamon and Arcite.

The younger Knight had ridden back into the town, and on the morrow, before daybreak, having secretly provided two complete equipments of armour, ready for their contest, he rode forth alone, carrying the whole on his horse before him. In the grove and at the time and place appointed they met. The colour fled from their faces at the first exchange of looks:—like a Thracian hunter, who stands in a gap with his spear, waiting for the roused bear or lion, and hears him coming through the underwood, crushing boughs and leaves in his passage, and thinks, 'Here comes my mortal enemy, whom without fail I must kill, or he will take my life:' so it was with these from the moment either caught sight of the other. No salutation, no compliment, passed at meeting, but each helped to arm his antagonist as friendly as he would his own brother; and then, with their sharp strong spears they long lashed and strove for victory. Palamon fared in the fight like a raging lion, and Arcite a hungry tiger. They rushed together with the obstinate fury of wild boars, panting and foaming, while the blood flowed to their feet. And so I leave them fighting while I bring you the news of Theseus.

This famous King had so great a love for hunting, that scarcely the day dawned which did not find him ready with hounds and horn to follow the stag of largest limb: it was his chief delight. Having fulfilled his duty to the god of battle, he joined the train of Diana.

On this same day, then, Theseus, with his Queen Ippolita, and the fair Emily, all clad in green, had ridden forth to the chace, and towards this very grove where he had heard of some game. He therefore made for an open plain through which the deer was wont to take flight, and over a brook, and so right on his way. When the King had arrived at this open space, he looked under the level beams of the morning sun, and beheld the combatants, like two bulls fighting furiously. Their bright swords glanced to and fro like lightning, and fell with hideous might. He, ignorant of their quality, put spurs to his horse, and at a start was between them both. 'Ho!' cried he, drawing his sword, 'no more, on pain of death. By mighty Mars, he that strikes another blow does it with penalty of his head. But say, who are ye, who are thus boldly fighting here, as if in the actual lists, without judge or other officer?'

To whom Palamon answered hastily:—'Sir, there need few words. We have both deserved death: we are two unfortunate wretches burthened with our lives; as, therefore, you are a just judge, grant us neither refuge nor mercy. Slay me first, but let him follow—or rather let him first die; for, though you little know it, this is Arcite your mortal foe, whom you banished from Athens: this, his return, alone, merits death. This same Arcite came to your gate and passed under the name of Philostrate. For years has he put this deceit upon you; he has been promoted to be your chief Squire, and presumes to love the fair Lady Emily. And since the day is come that I myself shall die, I plainly confess that I am that woful

THE KNIGHT'S TALE.

'Then did the Queen, the Lady Emily, and their train, in their womanly hearts, begin to weep. * * * And when they looked upon their gaping wounds, they implored his mercy upon their knees, till his mood began to soften.'

Palamon who has just broken from bondage—your mortal enemy, and the devoted lover of the Lady Emily, in whose sight and service I could at this moment yield my breath. Give me therefore present judgment and death; yet let not my companion go free, for both merit this reward.'

The King answered him, 'This matter has been quickly concluded: the confession of your own mouth has condemned you, and it shall be so recorded. You shall not, however, die the felon's death, but by the blood-red Mars, the sword shall fulfil your destiny.'.

Then did the Queen, the Lady Emily, and their train, in their womanly hearts, begin to weep; for they thought it a grievous chance to befall two gentlemen of so high estate, whose only misfortune was, that they had loved too well. And when they looked upon their gaping wounds, they implored his mercy upon their knees, till his mood began to soften (for pity soon finds its way to the noble heart); and though he at first trembled for wrath, yet when he shortly considered with himself the cause of their trespass, his reason excused them, however his anger had chafed at their offence. He thought that every man will, if possible, help himself in love; and that he will seize the chance of escape from prison. Moreover, he had compassion on the weeping women, and he concluded that it were a shame to a lord of gentle heart, who will have no mercy, but still maintains a lion-heart both in word and deed, as well towards him who repents, as to the unrelenting man that stiffly maintains his first determination: he can have little discretion who would confound pride and humility. When therefore the clouds of his anger had passed away, he looked up with light and beaming eyes, and thus addressed the assembly.

'Hail to the mighty God of Love!—nothing can withstand his power. The wonders he achieves proclaim him a God, for he makes all hearts subservient to his will. This Palamon and Arcite, who had wholly escaped from my prison, have lived here, in Athens, knowing me to be their mortal enemy, and that their lives were in my power; yet hath love, in spite of their heads, brought them both here to die.

Who but a fool would be in love? Look at their wounds, see how they bleed: thus hath the god they worship rewarded them for their service: and yet they, in their wisdom, will obey his dictates, happen what may. But the greatest folly of all is, that she, for whom there has been all this hot fare, knew as little of it as myself. But, young or old, man will at one time be a fool. As I have myself, however, in times past, engaged in the same service, and know the sore straits to which one may be brought through love, I here, at the request of my kneeling Queen, and dear sister Emily, wholly acquit you, Knights, of your trespass; and, in return, you both shall swear to me that you will never more disturb my dominion by night or by day, but, to your utmost, be my friends and allies.' They accepted his oath, and in granting their pardon he thus said to them:

'As regards my sister Emily, on whose account you maintain this jealousy and strife, though she were a Queen or Princess, either of you, by virtue of royal descent or wealth, is worthy to wed her. Since, however, she can marry but one, and that the other must be doomed to pipe his loss under an ivy leaf, each of you shall abide the fate destined for him, and after the following fashion. You shall go forth freely wherever you list, without ransom or danger from me; and by this day fifty weeks, each shall have collected from far and near a hundred Knights, armed 'all in proof' for the lists, ready to contend in battle for the hand of the lady: and this promise I hold you upon the truth of my knighthood, that whichever shall slay his opponent, or drive his hundred from the lists, on him will I bestow the hand of Emily to wife.'

Who was now light of heart, but Palamon? who bounded for joy but Arcite? and who can describe the rejoicings which were made when Theseus granted this fair favour? All, as well as the two Thebans, went on their knees and thanked him with grateful hearts. And so blithely the Knights took leave, and rode homeward towards old Thebes.

I must not omit to recount the great expense at which Theseus erected the lists. A nobler theatre I may say the world never beheld. It was a full mile in circuit, walled with stone, and without the wall ran a moat. The shape was circular, with seats all round, sixty feet in height, raised one above another, so that no one could deprive his neighbour of beholding the spectacle. Eastward and westward in the circle was erected a gate of white marble. Every craftsman and artisan, even to the sculptor of images, was employed by Theseus to raise and adorn this structure; so that in the like space the earth did not contain so fair a theatre. Upon the east gate were raised an altar and an oratory to Venus, the Goddess of Love; and upon the western one another in honour of Mars: northward also, in a turret on the wall, was a rich oratory of alabaster and white and red coral, in worship of Diana the chaste.

Nor should I leave out the noble carving and the paintings in these three oratories. First, in the temple of Venus might be seen displayed upon the wall, personified in piteous array, the broken sleeps, cold sighs, the sacred tears and lamentings that love's servants endure in this life: pleasure, hope, desire, foolhardiness, youth and beauty, riches, jealousy, and flattery; feasting and dancing, carols and instruments, and many more than I can enumerate. And there was painted her famed dwelling on Mount Citheron: nor were forgotten the histories of fair Narcissus, the folly of King Solomon, Hercules' might, the enchantment of Medea and Circe, the fierce courage of Turnus, or the base servitude of Crœsus. The figure of the goddess, glorious to behold, was seen naked floating in the wide sea: half her form hidden by the bright green waves. In her hand she bore a harp, and on her head a fresh garland of roses: above it were her doves hovering. Before her stood her son Cupid, winged and hoodwinked. He carried a bow with bright and keen arrows.

The interior of the mighty Mars' temple was painted like the famous one in Thrace, that frosty region where the god holds his chief dwelling. First upon the wall was depictured a forest, that harboured neither man nor beast, full of old barren trees, gnarred and stubby; through which a storm was roaring as if it would crash every bough. At the bottom of a hill stood the temple of the god, wrought of tempered steel, the entrance to which was long, narrow, and dreary. The light shone in at the door, for there were no windows. The door was of adamant, clamped with iron, and the pillars were iron, massive and shining.

There was to be seen the dark imagining and completion of Felony; cruel Wrath, red as a conflagration; pale Fear; the Smiler with the knife under his cloak; buildings in flame; murderings treacherously in bed; open war; ghastly wounds; contention with its sharp menace, and bloody knife. There was the suicide, his hair bathed in gore; and cold death, with the mouth upright, gaping. In the midst of the temple, and over all, sat Mischance, with sorry aspect. Madness was also there, laughing in his rage; injustice, complaint, and fierce outcries: the tyrant with his prey carried off by force: the town destroyed, and nothing left.

The statue of Mars, armed and of grim aspect, was standing upright in a chariot, and at his feet was a wolf, with fiery eyes, eating the body of a man.

And now to finish shortly with the Temple of the chaste Diana. The walls were adorned with deeds of hunting and shamefaced chastity. There was the unfortunate Calistope, whom for wrath Diana changed into a bear, and afterwards she became the polar star. Dane, also, turned to a tree. Acteon, too, changed by Diana to a deer, in punishment for his having seen her naked. His own hounds were worrying him, not knowing that he was their master. Then followed the description of Atalanta hunting the wild boar, with Meleager, and many besides, for which Diana wrought them sore affliction.

The Goddess was seated on high upon a hart, surrounded by a pack of hounds, and underneath her feet was the moon. Her statue was clad in bright green; and she had a bow in hand with a quiver of arrows. Her eyes were bent downwards towards the dark region of Pluto (of which dominion she was also queen). A woman in labour lay before her, imploring the aid of Lucina.[1]

---

[1] Diana, when presiding over childbirth, passed under the name of Lucina.

The lists, with the temples and theatre being finished at a great cost, I will leave speaking of Theseus for a time, and turn to Palamon and Arcite.

The day draws near for their returning, when each should bring his hundred knights to Athens to try the battle, as I have already said. Those who accompanied Palamon were variously appointed according to their several fancies. Some were clad in a light coat of mail, with a short cassock and breastplate: some in two simple plates of armour, and a shield: others well defended their limbs, and were armed with an axe, or mace of steel. In his train also was seen Lycurgus, the great King of Thrace, of manly aspect, with thick black beard and piercing eyes, that glowed in his head like stars. He was large of limb, broad-shouldered, and his arms were round, long, and firm. Aloft upon a golden chariot he stood, drawn by four white bulls, and as he passed along he looked about him like an eagle. Instead of coat-armour he wore a bear-skin, coal-black. His long hair flowed behind his shoulders and shone against the sun like a raven's wing. A golden coronet of enormous weight, studded with diamonds and rubies, circled his brows. About his chariot went twenty or more mastiff-hounds that he employed in lion-hunting. They followed in leashes, muzzled, and collared with golden collars. A hundred lords were in his company, armed cap-à-piè and stout of heart.

The great Emetrius, King of India, accompanied Arcite. He came riding like the God Mars, upon a bay steed clad in steel, covered with cloth of gold: the saddle was inlaid with finely wrought gold. His coat armour was made of silk, trimmed with fair large pearls; and from his shoulders hung a short mantle thickly embroidered with rubies glowing like fire. His crisp yellow hair danced in ringlets around his neck like sunbeams. He had a high and arched nose, eyes of a bright hazel colour; full and round lips, and a sanguine complexion. Moreover, his face was sprinkled with a few freckles of a mingled dark and light yellow hue. His manner of looking round him was like that of a lion. His beard was young and vigorous, (he appeared to be about five and twenty years of age,) and the tone of his voice pierced the air like a trumpet. He was crowned with a fresh and lusty garland of laurel; and upon his fist sat a tame eagle, purely white as a lily. A hundred knights attended him, all richly caparisoned, and, save their heads, in complete armour: for earls, dukes, and kings joined in this train through love, and for the increase of chivalry. Tame lions and leopards also gamboled around the royal car. After such fashion and order, did all these nobles arrive at the city early in the morning, and alight within its walls.

Theseus entertained them, each according to his rank, with full honour and knightly courtesy. If I did not wish to bring you to the effect and point of my tale, I would describe to you all the service at the high feasting; the minstrelsy; the rich present and the largess to both high and low; the appointment and rich array of the palace; the falcons disposed around on their perches, and the hounds lying here and there upon the floor, quietly expecting the feasters' casual superfluity: I would tell you of the fairest dames, and the best dancers; the songs, the gallantry, and the more earnest love-making.

Before daybreak, and as soon as the lark had begun to sing, Palamon, with a devout and courageous heart bent his steps towards the Temple of Venus that was erected in the lists: where he knelt down and besought her help to gain him possession of his Lady Emily, in whose service he fain would die. 'And if, O Goddess! mine,' said he, 'thou grant that I may have my love, I will evermore worship in thy temple, and offer daily sacrifice upon thine altar. But if thou turn thy face from me, lady sweet! I pray that on the morrow Arcite's spear may cleave my heart; for, my life being gone, I reck not his better fate in winning her to wife.' When his prayer and sacrifice were concluded, the statue of the Goddess shook, and made a sign, which, although somewhat delayed, he accepted as a boon that his prayer had been heard favourably: so home he went, light of heart.

At sunrise Emily arose, and attended by her maidens, went forth to the Temple of Diana; taking with them the fire, and the incense, the garments, and the horns of mead fit to perform sacrifice. The preparation for the holy ceremony, by the purifying of her body at a wellspring, being attended to, and the sacred place being fumed with odorous gums, the maiden princess (gentle and debonair of heart) having her head crowned with a garland of oak, and her bright hair untressed, and flowing down her back, proceeded to kindle two fires on the altar. After, she addressed the goddess of the green woods, the protectress of maidenhood, and queen of the deep dark realm of Pluto. 'O chaste Goddess!' said she, 'thou knowest the desire of my heart, that I should all my days remain a maiden, taking delight in the wild woods and the cry of the hunters. Help me now, lady queen of night, since thou canst help; send peace between this Palamon and Arcite, who now strive for love of me. Quench the busy torment and fire of their hearts, and turn their love towards another. Behold, O Goddess of clean chastity, and consider the tears upon my cheeks: I would still follow in thy train, and end my life a maiden in thy service. But if my destiny have so befallen, that I am doomed to be the wife of one, then grant me him who most sincerely loveth me.'

While she was in her prayer the fires upon the altar were burning clearly : but, suddenly, a strange sight arose to her view ; one of the fires sank, and kindled again; the other became extinct, with a whistling noise like the burning of moist brands, and at their ends ran forth as it were drops of blood. Emily, aghast at the sight, shrieked like one distracted, not knowing how to divine the manifestation of the oracle. At this moment the Goddess herself appeared, with her bow in hand and dressed like a huntress. 'Daughter,' said she, 'stay thy sorrow. The eternal word of the great Gods hath confirmed that thou shalt be wedded to one of those who for thy sake have undergone so much care and pain. To which of them I may not tell thee. The fires upon the altar have already signified the conclusion and manner of thine adventure.'

Thus having spoken, at the quick clattering of her quivered arrows, she vanished from the view of the astonished Emily, who, placing herself under the protection of the Goddess, returned home pondering the mystery of the oracle and of the vision.

Closely following upon Emily, Arcite went to the Temple of Mars to perform his sacrifice. Having finished all the rites, he intreated the God of arms, whom he constantly served, to grant him the victory on the ensuing day; in the event of which he vowed to offer at his shrine his flowing hair and beard, that had never felt the edge of shears or razor. 'This will I dedicate to thee, O! strong God of arms! together with my banner, and the accoutrements of all my company, which I will hang up in thy temple, and until the day of my death will I burn before thee eternal fire upon thine altar.'

His petition being ended, the rings upon the temple doors clattered, the fire upon the altar burned with a strange brightness, and a sweet smell steamed forth from the ground:— when in acknowledgment of the omen, having cast fresh incense upon the flame, and performed other rites, the statue of the god rang upon his hauberk, after which a low dim sound murmured ' Victory !'

Arcite gave glory and honour to Mars, and returned home as glad as a bird is of the bright sun.

This day was passed in Athens in great feasting, jousting, and dancing: but as the revellers were to rise early on the morrow to behold the fight, they were early at rest. And by day-spring in the morning, the noise of horses and harness was heard in every quarter; and lords upon their palfreys were thronging to the palace.

There might be seen the arranging of armour, uncommon and rich, wrought with steel and goldsmithry; bright shields, head-pieces, trappings, golden helmets, hauberks, and coat-armoury; lords in gay furniture on their coursers; knights and squires in retinue: the fixing of spear-heads, and buckling of helmets, polishing of shields, and lacing of thongs: foaming steeds, gnawing their golden bits. The armourers, too, riding hither and thither with files and hammers 'to accomplish the knights;' yeomen on foot, and commoners in throngs with short staves: pipes, trumpets, and clarions, that blow the bloody sounds of war; the palace full of people driving to and fro, or standing in dozens, discussing the merits of the Theban knights; some favouring him with the black beard, others with the thick; the one they said had a fierce look, and would fight bravely; and that the other wielded an axe of twenty pounds weight.

Thus was the hall full of surmises and conjectures long after sun-rise. The great Theseus, who had been awakened by the music and the thronging, remained in private till the two Theban knights had been brought to the palace, and both received due and equal honours.

The King was seated at a window, and looked like a god enthroned. When the people had assembled round, a herald commanded silence, and thus signified the royal will.

'To prevent the needless destruction of gentle blood by fighting after the manner of mortal battles, the King decrees that no man, upon pain of death, shall take into the lists any halberd, short sword, or knife; that no one shall ride more than one course, with a sharp spear, against his antagonist; that if he choose, he may defend himself on foot; and anyone who by mischance shall be taken alive, and brought to the stake, agreed upon by both sides, shall remain there till the strife be concluded: and lastly, if the chieftain on either side be taken or slain, the tournament shall straightway cease.'

Up went the trumpets, with their rousing tones; and the whole company rode forth to the lists, which were hung all round with cloth of gold. Theseus went first, and on either side the two Thebans: the Queen and Emily followed, and after them the company, according to their rank.

When these were all seated, the populace crowded in, and were ranged in order. Then from the west gate, under Mars, entered Arcite and his hundred partisans, bearing a red banner:—at the same moment, on the east side, under Venus, and bearing a white banner, Palamon entered, with confident and courageous bearing. Never were two companies so matched, both in worthiness of deeds, estate, and age. After they had been arranged in order, and their names called over to prevent the taking of undue advantage, the gates were shut, and the cry was made—'Now, young and proud Knights, do your duty.'

The heralds ceased riding up and down; and now the trumpets and clarions sound to the charge. In went the spears sadly[1] to their rests, and the sharp spurs were dashed into the horses' sides. Now might be seen shaft handles shivered upon the bucklers, and spears whirled aloft into the air. Out flew the swords, gleaming like polished silver, and helmets were hewn or rolled upon the earth. Some force their passage through the thickest ranks with mighty maces, smashing skulls and limbs. Here lay one stark dead, pierced to the heart; another sobbing out his life with the stern tide of blood. The strongest chargers are overthrown; and men and horses are hurtling together upon the ground, in mad confusion.

Frequently during the conflict the two Thebans encountered; and like wild beasts

---

[1] Firmly, fixedly.

bereft of their young, or mad with hunger, thirsted for each other's blood. But while they were engaged, the King Emetrius seized hold of Palamon, whose sword had made a bitter wound in Arcite's flesh, and with the strength of twenty men was dragging him to the stake: Licurgus, in rushing to his rescue was borne down; and Emetrius himself, notwithstanding all his might, was borne a sword's length from his saddle by a blow from Palamon, before he could be taken. Yet all in vain—his hardy heart could not bestead him, and he was brought by force to the stake.

When Theseus beheld this event, he arose and put an end to the conflict, declaring that Arcite of Thebes had won the fair Emily. At this, the shouting of the multitude burst forth, and seemed to rock the lists to their foundations. When the noise of these, the sounding of the trumpets, and the proclamation of the heralds had ceased, a wondrous event happened which changed the fortune of the victor.

As Arcite, with his helmet off to show his face, was pacing down the lists, and looking upward at his prize, the lovely Emily,—who on her side, by a favouring glance, gave him to heed that she was all his own, both in heart as well as by the fortune of battle,—suddenly a fury, sent from the infernal regions by Pluto, started out of the ground before his horse, which made him leap aside for fear; and foundering as he leaped, Arcite was thrown upon his head, and his breast was crushed with the saddle-bow. Being carried to the palace of Theseus, and his armour cut off, he was softly laid upon a bed; the name of Emily all the while hanging upon his lips.

Meantime the King, with all his company, returned to the city, and were feasted by him three days; during which time the wounded were dressed; and when the time for parting arrived, he accompanied them a long journey from his town, everyone turning his own way home.

Arcite's injury continued to increase, for the inward bleeding could not be stopped on account of the bursting of the blood-vessels in his lungs. When he found that his death was near, he sent for Emily and his dear cousin, Palamon, and addressed to them the following tender and noble farewell.

'My woful heart cannot declare to you the sum of the sorrows it has endured in your behalf, my best beloved lady! but I bequeath to you, above all the world, my spirit's service, since my life here may no longer remain. Alas the woe! alas the sharp trials that I have so long suffered for you! alas the death! alas my Emily! alas the departing of our company! alas, queen of my heart! alas my wife! lady of my heart! closer of my days!—What is this world? and what doth man desire?—now with his love, and now in his cold grave—alone—without any company. Farewell, my sweet! farewell my Emily!—And now, for the love of heaven, take me softly in your arms, and hearken to what I say.

'For a long time I have been at strife and rancour with my cousin Palamon here, and all through love and jealousy on your account: now, Jove guide my mind to speak properly and truly of a rival, and with all circumstance: that is to say, with a feeling of all that belongs to truth, honour, and knighthood, wisdom, humility, estate, and lofty kindred; so Jove receive my spirit, as I know no man now in this world so worthy to be beloved as my cousin Palamon, who has served you, and will do till his death: if therefore you ever resolve to become a wife, do not forget Palamon the gentleman.'

And with that word his speech began to fail; for the chill of death was rising from his feet up to his breast. His arms too were losing their vital power; the intellect alone remained, when his sighing heart began to fail with the sense of death: his breath shortened, his eyes became dim, yet still he kept them fixed on her;—and his last words were, 'Mercy! Emily!'

Theseus bore his fainting sister from the corpse. Palamon wept; and all the city lamented the untimely death of this unfortunate and brave young knight.

In due time the King gave orders for the funeral, and commanded that the ceremony should be performed at that same grove where he and Palamon had striven for love of Emily. A funeral pile was raised of many trees, felled for the purpose; and upon a bier, covered with cloth-of-gold, Arcite was laid, (his face uncovered,) clad in a suit of the same material. His head was crowned with green laurel; his white gloves were upon his hands, and one of them held his own good sword.

Then came the mourner Palamon, with dishevelled hair and beard, in a black suit bedropped with his tears, and, excepting Emily, the ruefullest of the train.

After these came three steeds, caparisoned with glittering steel, adorned with the arms of Arcite. Their riders bore his shield, his spear, and his bow, the case and furniture of which were of burnished gold. They rode forth towards the grove at a solemn pace. The bier was supported upon the shoulders of the noblest Greeks; and the great street of the city through which they passed was hung with black. Theseus, accompanied by old Egeus, followed the train, bearing golden vessels containing honey, milk, blood, and wine. Emily, in accordance with the custom of the time, carried the fire for the funeral service. I need not tell you all that was done at the ceremony. Of the felling of the trees, of the spicery and the garlands, the myrrh and the incense: how Arcite lay among all this; nor what store of costliness was heaped about his body; and how Emily set fire to the pile; nor what she said, nor how she swooned; nor of the jewels, the shields, the spears, and the vestments, the cups of wine, and milk, and blood which were cast into the fire; nor how the Greeks with loud shouts rode three times round the pile on the left hand; three times clashing their spears; or the three wails of the women; the burning of the body to ashes, and the funeral games of the Greeks when all was over. Therefore, to bring my long story to an end: After a decent process of time, when the mourning for Arcite had ceased, Theseus sent for Palamon, who, unmindful of the cause, appeared in his sable dress. Emily also came at the same message. After fixing his eyes upon them for some time, and that all the company was hushed, he made a grave discourse, which he concluded in the following manner. 'Why are we sad, that good Arcite, the flower of chivalry, has departed with high honour from the thraldom of life? Why do his wife and cousin here regret his welfare?—they who loved him so well. My purpose before we leave this place, is, to convert this double sorrow into a perfect and lasting joy: and therefore, dear sister, with the assent of my whole council here, it is my full wish that your own knight, the gentle Palamon, who, from the time he first saw your face, hath served you with good will and faithful heart, receive your favour and become your lord and husband. He is son to a King's brother, and therefore not unworthy of you: but if he were no more than a poor bachelor, since he hath served you for so many years through sharp adversity, you should consider and recompense his deserts. Give me here your hand.' Then turning to Palamon, he said, ' Methinks, there is little need to entreat your assenting to my purpose. Draw near and take your lady by the hand.'

Then was the bond of marriage drawn up by the council, and Palamon wedded his Emily. Long did he live in bliss, health, and riches; Emily loving him tenderly, and he serving her with so much gentleness, that no word of strife or jealousy was ever heard between them.

So ends the history of Palamon and Arcite; and God save all this fair company.

THE MAN OF LAW'S TALE.

PROLOGUE.

Our worthy host perceived by the altitude of the sun that it had performed one quarter of its day's journey: so, suddenly turning his horse round, he said:—'My masters! it is already ten o'clock; my advice therefore is, that you lose no time, but get forward on your journey. Time is ever on the wane, and steals away from us, both while we sleep, and during our waking hours of negligence—as the mountain stream never returns from the plain to its source. Sir Man of Law, since you have consented to submit to my judgment, now tell your tale according to agreement:—abide by the summons, and you will at least have acquitted yourself of your duty.'

'Mine host,' said he, 'I have no intention to break my covenant:—duty is a debt, and I cheerfully perform my best—I can say no more: for the law by which man restrains his fellow, he himself should abide by. Certain it is, however, that I can tell you no tale of merit, that this rogue Chaucer has not been beforehand with me: for, in one book or another, he has told more love-stories than Ovid himself, the great master of the art. Nevertheless, I care not, though I do come limping with my prose after his rhymes.' Having thus spoken, he in a sober style began the following tale.

THE STORY OF THE LADY CONSTANCE.

In Syria, in former days, there dwelt a company of rich merchants, who exported far and near their cloth-of-gold, rich satins, and spicery: their merchandise was so rare and excellent, that all were eager to deal and barter with them. Now it happened that some of these traders turned their course towards

Rome, and remained there as long as suited their pleasure and convenience. During their stay they heard of little but the great renown of the Emperor's daughter, the Lady Constance. The common talk of every one was; 'Our Emperor—God preserve him—has a daughter, such as, for goodness and beauty, the world never saw surpassed. She possesses beauty without pride; youth without folly or inexperience:—in all her actions, virtue is her guide. In her, humility has overcome tyranny: she is the mirror of gentleness and courtesy: her heart is the very shrine of holiness; and her hand the minister of freedom in almsgiving.'

After these merchants had freighted their ships, and obtained a sight of this gifted maiden, they made their way back to their native country.

It happened that these merchants were in high favour with the Sultan of Syria; who, when they returned from foreign and strange places, would courteously entertain them, and eagerly gain from them intelligence respecting the various kingdoms they had traversed, and the novelties they had observed. Among other matters, the travellers detailed so seriously the great beauty and virtue of the Lady Constance, that the Sultan was unable to dismiss her from his thoughts, but fell in love upon the bare report of her surpassing excellence. Whereupon he summoned his privy council, and commissioned them to ease his heart by devising a plan which should obtain for him in marriage the hand of the Lady Constance. Many were the arguments and the difficulties raised by the counsellors; among others, the great diversity in the religious institutions of the two countries: for they rationally concluded that no Christian prince would wed his child with a follower of Mahomet.

This objection, however, he overruled by declaring, that rather than be separated from her, he would himself become a Christian.

There is no occasion to detail all the account of the treaties and embassies which passed between the two courts: suffice to say, it was agreed that the Sultan and his chief nobles should receive baptism and embrace Christianity; and that the Lady Constance should be bestowed in marriage upon the former, with I know not what portion of gold by way of dowry.

Bishops, and other holy men, with lords, ladies, and knights, were appointed to attend in her train. Moreover, public prayers were offered through the city, that this marriage might be acceptable in the sight of heaven, as well as for the preservation of the travellers on their perilous voyage.

The day arrived for their departing—the woful day!—and all were prepared. Constance, who was overcome with sorrow, arose with pale and anxious face and made ready to depart; for so the event was to be. Alas! no wonder she wept:—a gentle and tender creature to be sent away from friends by whom she had been carefully nursed, to sojourn among strangers in a strange country, and become subject to the will of one she knew not.

'Father,' said she, 'your wretched child, Constance,—your young daughter, so softly fostered,—and you, my mother, my sovereign delight above all things in this world; Constance, your child, recommends herself to your frequent prayers. I shall go into Syria, and you will never more behold my face;—since it is your will, alas! that I must go to this barbarous nation: but HE, who suffered for our redemption, give me grace to fulfil all his commands. For me, wretched creature! no matter though I perish. Women are born to thraldom and penance, and to be subjected to the dominion of man.

When Pyrrhus rased the walls of Troy and burned the town; when Thebes was levelled with the ground; when Hannibal three times overcame the Romans, there was not heard more piteous weeping than in this chamber at the parting of Constance.

This fair and woful maid was brought to the ship with every circumstance of solemnity. 'Now, Jesus, our heavenly Saviour, be with you all,' she said. There was no more, but,— 'Farewell, fair Constance!' she all the while striving to put on a cheerful face. In this manner she sailed away; and now I will turn to another part of my story.

The mother of the Sultan, who was a fountain of every vice and treachery, having discovered her son's intention to cast off his old religion, suddenly and privately summoned her privy council, whom she thus harangued.

'My Lords, you are all apprised that my son is on the point of deserting the holy laws of our Koran, dispensed to us by Mahomet the Prophet of God. As respects myself, however, I here vow to that great God, that life shall rather depart from this body than the laws of Mahomet from my heart. What are we to expect from this new faith but thraldom and penance to our bodies here; and for our backsliding from Mahomet, hell hereafter? Yet, my Lords, if you will pledge me your assurance to abide by my counsel, I shall fully provide for our future safety.'

Every man assented, and swore to live and die with her. Each one also promised to exert himself to strengthen her cause by every influence in his power. This compact being settled, she thus explained the enterprise she had taken in hand.—' First, we will feign to embrace Christianity—a little cold water will not harm us. Then I will ordain such a feast and revelry as, if I mistake not, will prove an ample requital to the Sultan. As for his wife, though she be christened pure and white as morning milk, she will need a whole font of water to wash away the red stains of that hour.'

This Sultaness—this root of iniquity, this serpent under woman's form—privately dismissed her council, to fulfil the agreement made with her, while she rode to the Sultan, and made confession to him of her repentance for having so long remained in the bonds of heathenism, with her resolution to renounce her faith, and at the priest's hands to embrace Christianity: entreating him at the same time that the honour might be granted her to entertain all the Christian strangers. The Sultan granted her request, thanking her at the same time on his knees for the mark of courtesy she had offered to his friends. He was so rejoiced he knew not what to say. She kissed her son, and returned home.

These Christians, a large and solemn company, at length arrived in Syria. The Sultan immediately dispatched a message to his mother, and to his court all around, informing them of his bride's arrival, requiring them, for the honour and dignity of his crown, to ride forth and meet the new queen.

The throng of mingled Syrians and Romans formed a rich array. The Sultaness, splendidly apparelled, received the young stranger as any mother would a beloved child. I know not whether the triumph of Julius, which Lucan has described so magnificently, were more remarkable than the assembly of this blissful company: but this scorpion of a Sultaness, notwithstanding her flattery and pleasant cheer, had concealed under all a deadly sting.

Soon after, the Sultan arrived in such royal pomp, that it was wonderful to behold, and with gladness of heart welcomed her to a second home; and so I leave them in the full enjoyment of mirth and bliss.

The time had now come when the old Sultaness had prepared the feast I spoke of, and had invited to it all the Christians, both young and old. There were they regaled with dainties and luxuries more than I can describe—

though all, alas! bought at a dreadful price. Too certainly does sudden woe succeed to worldly bliss: the end of the joy of our labour is sprinkled with bitterness, and grief follows in the train of mirth. For your security's sake, therefore, attend to this advice:—in the day of gladness think upon, and provide against the evil which comes up behind.

Shortly to describe this event:—the Sultan and every Christian were murdered at table, the Lady Constance alone being spared. The old Sultaness, with her friends, compassed this cursed deed, that she herself might rule the kingdom uncontrolled. Not even one Syrian of the Sultan's council who had been converted, escaped the frightful massacre: and Constance, who was wild with horror and dismay, they hurried into a vessel that had no rudder, bidding her find her way to Italy. A certain treasure she had brought to Syria, and store of provision, with clothing, they yielded to her; and forth she drifted on the salt sea. The ruler of all events be thy Pilot, gentlest and most forlorn of women! She blessed herself, and with a piteous voice prayed to the holy Cross. 'Oh bright, oh blissful altar!—holy Cross! red with the blood of the Lamb that washeth away the sin of the world; keep me from the snares of the Evil One in the day that the deep sea shall swallow me.'

Day after day—day after day the rising sun found this tender creature floating hither and thither upon the billows like an uprooted weed, throughout the Greek sea, to the Straits of Morocco: small and miserable was her fare; great and unceasing, whether awake or asleep, was her fear of death. If you ask why she was not drowned? or who preserved her at the feast? I answer, who saved Daniel in the horrible den of lions? when all, save him alone, were torn limb from limb. In Constance, the great and good God displayed a wonderful miracle, that his mighty works should be made known. For often by certain means, which to us appear dark, he accomplishes certain ends, that our ignorance and short sight cannot detect. She was preserved by a miracle, she was fed by a miracle, and so was she driven about the wide sea; till, at last, she was thrown ashore under a castle, far up on the coast of Northumberland, and her vessel remained so fixed in the sand that the flood-tide could not move it.

The constable of the castle came down to view the wreck, and having searched it over, found this solitary and woe-worn woman, together with the treasure she had brought away. In her language, which was a corrupted sort of Latin, she besought him to have pity upon her misery. The constable understood her speech, and brought her to shore; when she knelt down upon the sand, and thanked the Being who had preserved her through all her trials. By no means, however, could she be brought to tell who she was. Yet the constable and his wife took pity on her, and wept over the story of her sufferings. Moreover, so desirous was she to serve and please every one around her, that all loved her who had once looked in her face.

The constable and Dame Hermegild, his wife, with all the inhabitants of that country, were Pagans; but Hermegild had a deep affection for Constance; and Constance, so long and so earnestly prayed, with tears and bitterness, that Dame Hermegild was converted through her grace. No Christian dared to dwell in that country; the believers were compelled to fly before their Pagan conquerors; and the Christianity of Ancient Britain took refuge in the strongholds of the Welsh mountains. Yet were not the Christian Britons so exiled but that some few remained who secretly worshipped Jesus; and three of these were dwelling near the castle, one of whom was blind.

One bright summer's day, the constable, with his wife and Constance, were walking towards the sea, that was a few furlongs distant; and in their way they met this blind man, who was also bowed down with age and infirmity. 'In the name of Christ,' cried this blind Briton, 'Dame Hermegild, give me my sight again.' The Lady feared lest her husband should hear the sound of that name; till Constance made her bold, by bidding her, as a daughter of the holy church, perform the will of Christ. The constable, astonished at the sight, enquired how all this might be. Constance answered him, that it was done by the power of Jesus Christ, which can deliver those who believe, from the snares of the Evil One. And then she laid before him all the doctrine of our holy law; so that before even-song the constable was converted, and professed himself a true believer in Christ.

This worthy man was not lord of the place I have described, but he held it under Alla, King of Northumberland, who bore so strong a hand against the Scots. But this is not the matter of my story.—Satan, who is ever on the watch to entrap erring mortals, had cast an evil eye on Constance and her perfections, and sought to requite her for all her godly works. To this end he moved a young knight, dwelling near the castle, to love her with a foul and dishonest affection; which, when he found had no avail, (for no temptation could bring her to sin and shame,) the villainous heart of the youth, through spite and disappointment, compassed his thought to make her die a felon's death. Watching therefore his opportunity, while the constable was away, he crept privately by night to Hermegild's chamber, who, with Constance had both fallen asleep, weary with long waking and prayer. Softly he went to the bed-side of Hermegild, and, with the Devil's aid, at one plunge severed her throat: then laying the bloody knife by the Lady Constance' side, he went his way.

Shortly after the constable returned, and saw his wife mercilessly murdered, and by the Lady Constance was found the bloody knife. Here was piteous weeping and wringing of hands! and what, alas! could she say, whose wits were wild with woe and horror?

The whole circumstance of the disaster was laid before the King, together with all the detail of time and place, where Constance was discovered in the ship, which you have already heard. The heart of the King shuddered with compassion when he saw so benign a creature fall into trouble and misfortune; for, as a lamb brought to the slaughter, so stood this innocent before the King; the traitor knight at her side, and acting the part of accuser. Notwithstanding all, however, there was great murmuring among the people, who would not believe that she had done this great wickedness; for they had known her to be ever virtuous, and loving Hermegild as her own life. Of this, all, save the murderer, bore testimony. The King was strongly incited by this witness, and determined to enquire more deeply into the case, to search the truth of the matter.

Ill-fated Constance! no champion have you to defend your right; and, alas the day! little can you defend yourself. If HE who suffered for our redemption be not your strong champion on this day, guiltless must you die. Before the assembled court she fell upon her knees and cried aloud—'O immortal God! who preserved Susanna from false accusation; and O! merciful Virgin, to whose Son the angels sing Hosannas, if I be guiltless of this deed, grant me succour in this sharp hour of my trial.'—Have you not sometimes, in the midst of a crowd, beheld the pale face of him who has been leading to his death, without even the hope of reprieve; a face so ghastly that it could at once be known from all the rest?—So stood Constance, and looked around. You queens, and ladies, all, living in prosperity, think with ruth upon *her* state—think how *she* was bested:—an emperor's daughter, standing alone, with not a friend to whom she could pour out her complaint.

The King had such compassion upon her forlorn state (for the gentle heart ever leans to the piteous side) that the tears flowed from his eyes. 'Quickly, let a book be brought,' said he, 'and if this knight will swear that she slew this woman, we will yet consult who shall be our justice in this case.' A British book containing the gospel was produced, and on this book he made oath that she was guilty. Immediately an unseen hand smote him on his neck, so that he fell like a stone, and, in the sight of all, his eyes burst from his head. Then in the general audience a voice followed, saying: 'Thou hast slandered the guiltless daughter of Holy Church in high presence — thus hast thou done.' All, save Constance alone, stood aghast at this wonder, each in dread of the divine wrath. All who had wrongly suspected her made repentance; and, to conclude, the miracle, with the mediation of Constance, wrought upon the King and many more present, who were converted.

Alla instantly condemned the traitor knight to death; and Constance, notwithstanding all his untruth and perfidy, had pity on his fate. After this the King wedded Constance with great solemnity, and so this shining star of holiness became a queen. All rejoiced in the event but Donegild, the king's mother, a tyrannical and cruel woman: her wicked and proud heart was wrung at the thought of her son's marrying a creature whom no one knew, or whence she came, or what she was.

After the lapse of some months, the King, being compelled to march against his old enemies the Scots, committed his wife, who was in expectation of presenting him with a child, to the protection of a bishop and his friend the constable. The meek and humble Constance in due course of time, and while her lord was still away, brought into the world a son and heir, who was christened' Maurice. And the constable despatched a messenger with a letter to the King, informing him of the event. The messenger, however, thinking to gain for himself some advantage, rode strait to the queen dowager, and under show of diligence, with fair speech informed her that Queen Constance had brought forth a son. 'And this letter, madam, contains the intelligence which I am to convey to Scotland; if your Highness have any commands to His Majesty your son, I am your slave both night and day.' Donegild commanded him to remain all night, and that in the morning he should receive her despatches.

The messenger passed his time in eating and drinking till his wits were gone; so that, while he was snoring like a swine, his letters were secretly conveyed from his box, and another letter wickedly indited, to the following purport, was substituted for them. It described the queen to have been delivered of so horrible and fiend-like a creature, that no one in the castle was hardy enough to remain with it: moreover, that the mother had by her magic and sorcery betrayed herself to be a witch, and that the whole court avoided her company. The receipt of this letter was a bitter stroke to the King, yet he made no one acquainted with his sorrows; but with his own hand returned for answer that he welcomed the will and ordinance of Heaven. 'For all this, however,' continued the letter, 'keep the child, be it foul or fair, and my wife also till my return home. The Saviour whom I serve will send me an heir, more agreeable than this, at his own good will.' This letter he sealed, secretly weeping, and sent it to the messenger, who set forth on his return home.

Having arrived at the Court of the Queen Mother, that fiend-like woman received him with much courtesy and favour, ordering him the same entertainments as before; and during his drunken sleep his letters were again stolen, and others, to the following purport, were substituted for them: viz.—that the King commanded his constable, upon pain of certain death, by hanging, not to suffer Constance to remain three days in his kingdom after receiving that order; but that she, with her infant son, and all the store she had brought with her, should be forthwith hurried into the same ship in which the constable had discovered her, and driven out from shore.

On the morrow the messenger made his way to the constable's castle, and delivered to him the letter: who, when he had read its contents, grievously lamented the bitter wickedness of the sentence, crying, 'Alas! alas! how can this world continue, so steeped in sin and cruelty is every creature!—Gracious God! if it be thy will, how can it meet the righteousness of thy judgment thus to suffer innocence to be betrayed, and wicked men to reign on in prosperity?—O! blameless Constance! deep is the measure of my grief, that I must either be your tormentor and your bane, or myself endure a shameful death!'

Both young and old in the neighbourhood wept at the news of this cursed letter; and on the fourth day Constance, with a deadly pale face, went toward the vessel: and kneeling down upon the strand, she said, 'Lord! ever welcome be thy decree;' and, she added, 'he that shielded me from blame while I was amongst you, can preserve me from harm in the wide sea. He is now as strong as he ever was: in Him I put my trust; He will be my sail and my load-star on the perilous deep.'

THE MAN OF LAW'S TALE.

'On the fourth day, Constance, with a deadly pale face, went toward the vessel; and, kneeling down upon the strand, she said: "Lord! ever welcome be thy decree."'

Her little child lay weeping on her arm:—
'Peace, peace, little son,' said she, 'I will not harm you:' with that she took her kerchief from her head and laid it over its little eyes, lulling the babe in her arm against her bosom; and, casting her eyes up to heaven, 'O, Mother!' she continued, 'blessed Virgin Mary! true it is that through a woman's tempting, mankind was lost, and doomed to perdition, for which error the flesh of thy Son was torn upon the cross: thy blessed eyes witnessed his torment; then is there no comparison between thine and any woe man may sustain. Thou sawest thy child slain before thine eyes—my little child yet liveth. O, blessed Virgin! to whom in their griefs all woful creatures turn; glory of womanhood! haven of refuge! bright star of day! look down with ruth upon my babe; thou who in thy gentleness lookest with pity on the miserable.

'O, little child! what, alas! has been thy guilt, that, as yet, can have wrought no sin? Why will thy cruel father shed thy life?'—and then she said, 'in mercy, dear constable, let my child dwell here with you:—yet, if you dare not preserve him from harm, in his father's name bestow upon him one kiss.' With that she looked backward toward the land, and said, ' Farewell, ruthless husband!' and then she arose and walked down the beach towards the vessel, the crowd following her, and she at intervals hushed her weeping babe. After blessing herself with devout intent, she took leave of all around, and stepped into the ship. The constable had taken good care to provide it with abundant store, and every necessary for a long voyage: and now may the Almighty God protect her, for she is driving away upon the sea.

Soon after this, King Alla returned home, and went strait to the castle, enquiring for his wife and child. At the sound of these words a sudden cold about the heart seized the faithful constable, who plainly laid before him the whole event, showing him at the same time the letter he had received, with his own seal affixed. The messenger was put to the rack till he had confessed distinctly where he had passed each night between his departure from Scotland and arrival at the royal castle. The hand that wrote the letter was discovered, with all the venom of this most cursed deed; and the effect of it was, that Alla, in the transport of fury, slew his own mother. Thus ended the ill-spent life of the traitress to her allegiance, old Donegild. But no tongue can describe the sorrow of Alla, who night and day bewailed the loss of his Constance and their child; while they for many a moon, through heat and cold, moist and dry, through many a windy storm and tempest, had been preserved, till her bark stranded, at last, under the walls of a heathen castle, the name of which I do not recall.

The people of the district came down, wondering at the appearance of the ship and at Constance; but during the night a steward of the castle came alone into the ship, with the intent of robbing the gentle voyager, and carrying her off. This wretched woman cried for help, and the child wept piteously, but her guardian, who was ever at hand, again brought her off unharmed, for in her struggle of despair the villain stumbled overboard and was drowned. The vessel afterwards was borne off by the tide, and drifted away again for many a weary day.

I must here change the thread of my story, and inform you of the Roman Emperor, who by letters out of Syria had received intelligence of the massacre of the Christians, with the dishonour offered to his daughter by the treacherous and murderous Sultaness, for which foul deed he sent forth a chosen senator, with other lords and picked troops, to take ample vengeance on those Syrians. They fulfilled their embassy with a loyal zeal, burning and destroying till wrath and justice were appeased. These fulfilled, the senator returned home crowned with victory, and in his voyage met the vessel driving, in which Constance was sitting, piteous and desolate. So changed was she in look and array, that he had not the slightest recollection of her, while she concealed her name and degree. He brought her home, however, with him to Rome, and placed her, with the little Maurice, under the care of his wife; who, though her aunt, was as ignorant of the quality of her guest as the senator himself.

After she had resided for some time in this manner, gladding the hearts of all around by her gentleness and good works, King Alla, her husband, came to Rome, for the purpose of doing penance, and to obtain pardon for the unholy deed of having slain his mother. The fame of his pilgrimage having been noised about the city, our senator, with his heralds and attendants, went forth to receive him, according to his quality. Each received the other with so much courtesy and good will, that the King invited the senator to a feast, who took the little Maurice with him, to behold the company and grandeur of the entertainment; and, by the instruction of his mother, during the intervals of the feasting, the child stood looking in the King's face. Alla fixed his eyes with wonder upon the boy, and said to the senator, 'Whose child is that standing yonder?' 'I know no more of him,' was the nobleman's answer, 'than that he has a mother, but, so far as I can hear, no father;' and with that he briefly rehearsed to the King how he found the child. 'But, Heaven knows,' added the senator, 'that in all my life I never met or heard of a more virtuous woman, maiden, widow, or wife, and I dare well say that she would go to death rather than commit a wicked deed.'

Now this child was as like to Constance as it was possible for one creature to resemble another. Alla remembered the face of Constance, and mused whether it might happen that the mother of the child was his own wife. With that thought he inwardly sighed, and hurried away from table. 'It must,' thought he, 'be the phantom of my brain; for my sober judgment would say my wife lies dead at sea; and yet, why may not the good God have guided Constance hither, as safely as he led her to my own country?'

After the feast, Alla went home with the senator to see the end of all this wonder; who sent hastily for Constance to come into the presence of the King: but when she knew the cause of the message, she could scarcely stand upon her feet. When Alla saw his wife, he embraced her eagerly and tenderly, weeping over her sweet and bitter tears: for at the first look he fixed upon her, he knew it was she;

while she stood dumb with sorrow, so closed was her heart in her distress when she remembered all his unkindness.. Twice she swooned in his arms, and he weeping, piteously excused himself. 'As Heaven shall have mercy on my soul,' said he, 'I am as guiltless of your harm as is my son here, Maurice—so like your own face.' Long was the sobbing, and the bitter pain, before their hearts could cease; but when it was finally known that Alla was guiltless of her persecution, they kissed a hundred times, and such bliss was between them that (unless it be the joy which will endure hereafter and for ever) no one has seen or ever will see the like.

She then meekly entreated her husband, in relief of her long sorrow, that he would especially beseech the Emperor to dine with him on a certain day, but on no account to make mention of herself. Some have it, that the child Maurice bore the invitation; but it should rather seem that Alla himself would perform that honour to the flower of all Christendom: yet the child went with him; and when the

Emperor had accepted the invitation, he looked steadily upon the face of Maurice, and thought upon his daughter.

The morrow came, and Alla with his wife prepared to meet the Emperor, riding out in gladness of heart to receive him; and when he drew near, she alighted, and throwing herself at his feet, said, 'Father,—Constance, your young and only child, is gone out of your remembrance. I am your daughter, your Constance, whom long ago you sent into Syria. I am she who was put alone upon the sea; who was condemned to death. Dear father! in mercy send me no more among the heathen; but receive and thank this Lord and King, *my* Lord, for all his kindness to me.' Who can describe the joy of those three, who had so strangely and happily met? And now to make a conclusion to my tale, this child, Maurice, was afterwards anointed Emperor by the Pope, and did high honour to the Christian church: —but my story is especially of Constance.

King Alla after due time returned to England with his sweet and holy wife, where they lived together in peace and happiness, although, alas! but for a short, though blissful season: happiness in this world is ever fleeting, and so it was with Alla and Constance; for, at the end of a year, death removed him from her; and she, in grief and heaviness at his loss, returned to the land of her birth. This divine creature travelled back to Rome, where she found her friends living and well. All her adventures had come to an end. And, weeping before her father's knees, with tender and sad thoughts, she returned thanks to God for her deliverance. Thus they lived in virtue and deeds of alms-giving, till they were separated for ever in this life. And now fare you well; my tale is over; and may HE who protected Constance, keep all here, and send them gladness after sorrow.

THE WIFE OF BATH'S TALE:

THE STORY OF
THE COURT OF KING ARTHUR.

In the days of the renowned King Arthur, whom Britons hold in high reverence, this land was peopled with fairies. The Elf Queen with her merry company have danced their roundels in many a green mead. What I speak of happened many hundred years ago: but now the elves are seen no more; for the charity and godly prayings of the begging friars who go sniffing into every corner of the land, as thick as motes in the sunbeams, bestowing their blessings on cities and towns, halls, chambers, and bowers, dairies and kitchens, are the cause that the fairies no longer remain: for where the elf was formerly, is now the friar, steadfastly paying his visits at morning and noontide meals, not forgetting his matins and benedictions as he makes his rounds of alms-begging. Now the women can safely walk abroad, through brake and copse, and sit under every green tree ; the friar is your only incubus,[1] and he will offer us no dishonour.

It happened that in the Court of this King Arthur dwelt a handsome and vigorous young bachelor Knight, who, on his return one day from a hawking party of water-fowl, saw before him a young maiden, whom in a transport of wilfulness and brutality he ill-treated. The unmanliness and violence of the deed raised such a clamour, and so keen a pursuit of the offender, that he was seized, tried, and condemned to lose his head. The Queen, however, and her ladies, so earnestly entreated his pardon of the King, that he granted him his life, and at the same time yielded him to his

---

[1] The *Incubus* was a fairy of less innocent character than his brethren. He succeeded the *Fauni* of the heathen mythology, and, like them, was supposed to inflict that oppression which goes under the name of *ephialtes*, or *night-mare*.

Queen, for her to order his penance:—who, turning to the ravisher, said, 'Such is your condition at this time, that you are in no surety of preserving your life: yet this will I grant, upon condition that you resolve me this question, '*What is that which women most desire?*' Beware! and think of your penalty. I allow you to depart for one twelvemonth and a day, to prepare your answer; and before you quit this presence you shall produce full security that at the given day you will yield yourself up to our decision upon your reply.'

The Knight was sorely perplexed with the condition of his sentence; so after much consideration, he resolved to leave the Court, and travel till the year's end; hoping that in the course of his adventures he might receive the help he required. From town to town, and house to house he went, wherever he thought to learn 'what women most desire:' but with all his pains he could not find two people of one mind in the matter. Some said, women love wealth better than anything else; some said honour; others, mirth; others again, splendour of dress; and some even thought their greatest pleasure lay in being often widowed and wedded. They came, perhaps, nearest to the truth who said that we are best pleased when we are flattered; for one and all of us (more or less) are soonest won by flattery. Attention and assiduity are the surest lime-twigs to our hearts. Some said, we most love to be free to follow our own inclinations; moreover, to be esteemed wise, and not to be reproved for our faults; for in truth, there is not one of the sisterhood who, if she be fretted on a tender point, will not turn again; and the more sharply for feeling that she deserves the rebuke. He who may make the trial will prove the truth of what I say. Be we never so faulty within, we *will* be held wise and free from offence. Some folks held the opinion, that we delight in being thought stedfast, firm of purpose, and close keepers of a secret; but that tale is not worth a straw; for we women can hide nothing:—witness the folly of Midas's wife;—will ye hear the story?

Ovid, among other traditions, has related that Midas had growing under his long shaggy hair two ass's ears, which he concealed so cleverly, that no one but his wife knew of the fact; and her he earnestly entreated to keep the secret of his disfigurement. She made oath to him that, for her own sake as well as his, she would not bring so great a shame upon her husband, even were it to gain the whole world. Notwithstanding all this, she was ready to expire with the pain of keeping this secret;—she had such a swelling of the heart, that some unlucky word she feared must necessarily slip out. Since, therefore, she dared tell it to no one, she ran down to a marsh hard by, her heart all on fire till she arrived there, and then like a bittern booming in the reeds, she laid her mouth down, and said, 'Betray me not, O water,—to you I tell it, and no one beside—my husband has two long ass's ears. And now is my heart at ease—the secret is out, for I could keep it no longer.' Thus you may perceive that, however stedfast we may remain for a time, out it must come at last; we cannot hide a secret. The remainder of the tale, if you desire it, is to be found in Ovid.

When this Knight, the hero of my story, found he was no nearer to the meaning of the

THE WIFE OF BATH'S TALE.

'The whole bevy of dancers had vanished, and no living soul was left behind, except a hideous old woman, bent double, and sitting on the green.'

riddle, he became very sorrowful; and the day having arrived when he must render up himself, he turned homeward. On his way, as he was riding by a forest-side, he perceived a company of more than twenty ladies dancing upon the grass; but as he eagerly drew near to them, hoping in his distress to gain some counsel from them, before he came up, the whole bevy of dancers had vanished, and no living soul was left behind, except a hideous old woman, bent double, and sitting on the green. This creature, more frightful than can be described, arose and went to meet the Knight; and she said, 'Sir Knight, this is no way to any place. Tell me, upon your faith, what it is you seek; it may, peradventure, be to your advantage: we old folk know, and can do much.'

'Certain it is, dear mother,' answered the Knight, 'that I shall be doomed to die, unless I am able to expound, "What it is that women most desire?" If you could instruct me I would amply repay you.'—'Pledge me your truth,' said she, 'here in my hand, that if it be in your power, you will perform the next act I require of you, and before night I will tell it you.'

'I accept,' said the Knight; 'and here is my truth.'—'Then,' said she, 'I dare boast that you are safe, for upon my life the Queen will say as I do. Let us see the proudest she that wears a kerchief, who will dare say nay to what I shall tell you. So, without farther parley, let us go forth.' She then whispered in his ear a short sentence, and bade him cheer up, and cast off all fear.

When they arrived at Court, the Knight said he had kept his word and the day for delivering up himself, and was ready with his answer. Many noble ladies had assembled to hear the sentence, the Queen sitting as judge, when the Knight was commanded to appear in Court: —and, silence being obtained, the question, 'What is it that women love best?' was put to him in due form and solemnity: when, in the audience of the whole Court, and in a bold manly voice, our knight answered; 'My Liege Lady, and most Royal Mistress,—what women desire above all things in this life is, to obtain dominion over their lovers and husbands, and in all matters to sway them to their will. This is the nearest and dearest thought of your hearts. Now, therefore, do with me as you list; I am in your power.' Throughout the whole Court there was not a woman, whether maid, wife, or widow, that contradicted him, and farthermore, they pronounced that he had fairly obtained his pardon.

At the moment the sentence was delivered, up started the old woman whom the Knight had seen sitting on the green-sward. 'Mercy! my sovereign Lady Queen,' said she, 'before this court break up, I entreat to have justice rendered to me. I taught the Knight this answer, for which he, at the time, plighted me his truth that he would grant me the first petition I might require at his hands, if it lay in his power to grant it.—Before this Court then, Sir Knight, I pray you to take me for your wife: I have preserved you from certain death;—if I speak falsely, upon your faith of knighthood gainsay my word.'

'Alas!' answered the Knight, 'such indeed was my promise: but for the love of heaven, I charge you to remodel your petition. Take all my wealth, but let me go free.'

'Nay, then,' said she, 'may a curse alight upon both of us, if I, though ugly, old, and poor, would not for all the gold above and beneath the earth, rather become your wife—aye! and your love too.'

'My love!' said he,—'my perdition! Oh! that any of my community should be so foully brought into contempt!'—All, however, was of no avail; he was compelled to wed this old woman, and take her to bed and board—'for better for worse.'

The joy, the display, and the feasting that was made upon the marriage of these two is soon told; for, in good sooth, there was neither joy nor feasting; but heaviness instead, and sullen sorrow. The Knight was married privately the next morning, and all the day, like an owl, hid himself for vexation at the deformity of his wife. And at night when they were in bed he tossed and tumbled about in disgust; the old woman all the while lay smiling by his side. 'My dear husband,' said she, 'does every gallant Knight treat his newly made wife in this kind and graceful manner?

Is this the custom of King Arthur's Court? Is every Knight in his train so sparing of courtesy and tenderness? I am your own love and your wife; I saved you from destruction; and, of a truth, never wronged you: why then behave thus to me? your conduct is like one insane. What is my crime—my offence? Tell me, and if I can, I will amend it.'

'Amend it!' said the Knight, 'No! no! you never can amend it. You are so old, so loathsome, and born of so low degree, that little should you wonder at my distress and horror. Would to heaven my heart would break at once!'

'Is this then,' said she, 'the cause of your uneasiness?'

'Certainly; and what wonder that it is.'

'Now, Sir,' said she, 'in three days, if I chose, I could amend all this, so that you would bear yourself towards me as you ought. But since you Knights speak of such high birth as is descended from ancient wealth, and presume that therefore you are *Gentlemen*;[1] I tell you

---

[1] The reader will recollect the note at page 111, explaining the original meaning of the word '*gentle*.'

that such arrogance is not worth a straw. He who secretly, and in the open face of day is most virtuous, who seeks to perform all the noble deeds in his power, is the most perfect gentleman. Jesus Christ commands that we claim our gentle birth from Him, who was "meek and lowly of heart;" not from our ancestors, because of their riches. For, though they leave us the whole of their inheritance, and to boast of our high kindred; yet can they not bequeath to us their virtuous lives which procured them the title of Gentlemen. Integrity of character seldom springs of its own accord in a man's descendants. We derive our gentle birth from the goodness of God only; from our ancestors we claim nothing but temporal benefits, which man may destroy. If gentleness of demeanour were implanted in a certain lineage, then would no one of that descent commit an act of villany. But we know that the sons of Lords will often shame their parentage. And he who demands praise of his gentility because he comes of a high family, having noble and virtuous ancestors, yet himself performs no deeds of gentleness, is no gentleman, duke or earl though he be; for deeds of villany constitute the base-born man. Gentility is but the renown of your ancestors on account of their signal goodness, and which is foreign to your individual self. Your gentility, like theirs, proceeds from God only. He is nobly born who performs noble deeds. Therefore, my beloved husband, I conclude that although my ancestors were rustic, yet, as I hope to live virtuously, then shall I become of gentle blood.

'And since you reprove me for my poverty, bear in mind that the Saviour of the world dwelt in wilful poverty; and the King of Heaven would not choose a vicious living. Cheerful poverty is doubtless an honest thing: and I hold him rich who considers himself repaid for his poverty in other gifts, although he have no shirt to his back: while the covetous man is really poor, for he would possess that which he cannot attain: but he who possesses nothing, yet covets nothing, is rich, although you esteem him but a knave.[1]

---

[1] The original meaning of the word *knave* is a hireling or servant.

The poor man may go on his way and have no dread of robbers. Poverty is a hateful good, though the redeemer from the cares of life: the improver of wisdom, to him who bears it patiently. Poverty makes a man know himself and his Maker too. It is a glass in which he may discover his true friends. Reprove me, therefore, no more for my poverty.

'As for my great age—though we had no written authority for the command—you men of gentle blood have ever held that age, in man or woman, is entitled to honour.

'And, to conclude, since I am loathsome as well as old, you will be in no danger that any one will seduce away your wife. Now, therefore, choose one of these two things:—to have me old and ugly till my death; to be to you a true and humble wife, and never to displease you during the whole course of my life: or to have me young and beautiful, and to take your chance of the temptation that will befall me from the great resort that will throng to your house on my account.'

The Knight bethought him,—sighed; and then said;—'My dear wife, I place myself under your wise direction: choose that which shall be most pleasant to yourself; at the same time befitting my honour as well as your own.'

'Then have I gained the mastery,' said she, 'since I may choose and govern according to my inclination!'

'Even so,' said he, 'I hold it best.'

'Now, then,' she replied, 'throw aside all your anger against me, and kiss me, for by my honour I will be to you both *beautiful* and *true*. Moreover, may I be utterly condemned, if I prove not as good and faithful a wife as ever this world saw; and, on the morrow, as fair to see as any Lady or Empress betwixt east and west. Draw the curtains, and behold half my promise.'

When the Knight saw the fulfilment of this marvel,—that she was both young and exceedingly handsome, for joy he took her in his arms, and kissed her a thousand and a thousand times. His heart was bathed in bliss; and so they lived to their lives' end; she obeying him in all things, and making his pleasure her happiness.

And so may we all have young and gentle husbands; and may such be quickly removed as will not be governed by their wives. As for your old and churlish niggards, Heaven reward them with a pestilence.

THE CLERK'S TALE.

PROLOGUE.

'Good Master Clerk of Oxford,' said our host, 'why, you ride there as still and coy as a young maid at her bridal feast! Not a word, I vow, has passed your lips the whole of this day. I would wager, now, that your brain is weaving some sophism or other: but as Solomon says, "There is a time for everything." So cheer up, man! *this* is no time for studying. You have consented to take a part in our play, and therefore, needs must be thinking of the character you have undertaken to perform. Come, then, tell us some merry tale; and for mercy's sake do not make it like a Lent sermon, bidding us bewail in sackcloth our sins and offences of the past year; or like many other sermons,—drone us to sleep. Give us a lively history of adventures; and, as for your colouring and rhetorical flourishes, keep them by you snug and warm till you are called upon to indite some high style, as when men address the presence of royalty. Upon the present occasion I would beseech you to be plain and simple in your matter, that the homely part of your audience may understand the whole of your discourse.'

Our worthy collegian courteously answered; 'Good host, I acknowledge your power and supremacy, and am prepared to obey you according to my ability. I will tell you a tale, which I learned at Padua, of a renowned and noble scholar and poet—the laureat PETRARCH, (now, alas! in his grave) who, with his choice rhetoric and poetry, illumined all Italy; as the famous LINIAN[1] did with his philosophy. But Death, "the common end of all, who will come when he will come," has snatched them both away, as it were in the twinkling of an eye.

---

[1] An eminent lawyer and philosopher, who lived in the fourteenth century.

'To return, however, to this great man (Petrarch) who taught me the story I propose relating to you, he has prefaced it in a high strain of eloquence by a description of the territory of Piedmont, with the rich district of Saluzzo, together with the swelling Appenines, that form the boundary of West Lombardy; including, in his account, the Mount Viso, from whose region the river Po, in a feeble spring, first takes its course eastward, towards the Emilian way, Verara and Venice, gaining strength and magnitude as it rolls along: all which, in the original work, however beautiful in itself, appears to me unconnected with the purpose in hand; except, indeed, that he skilfully contrives to make it lead to the matter of his history: and, therefore it is that I have slightly alluded to his description, because it forms the scene of the tale you are now to hear.'

THE STORY OF THE MARQUIS OF SALUZZO AND HIS WIFE GRISELDA.

On the west side of Italy at the foot of Mount Viso is situated a fertile plain, interspersed with thriving and populous towns, and fair castles, built ages ago. The name of this district is Saluzzo. It was formerly governed by a Marquis, who held his dominion by a long right of succession; and his subjects, both high and low, were bound in fealty to attend his summons, whether in war or peace. So discreet was he in his government (with one or two exceptions in his conduct) that he was beloved and feared by all, gentle and simple. He was a man of graceful person, vigorous constitution, in the prime of life, and full of honour and courtesy. His family was of so pure and noble a descent, that not one in all Lombardy could compare with him in gentleness of blood. The name of this young nobleman was Walter.

The indiscretions in his conduct to which I have alluded, were, that he was too prone to gratify the desires of the present moment, without regard to the future: and so great was his delight in hawking and hunting, that the graver cares and duties of life were not sufficiently regarded. But what, in the minds of his subjects, gave cause for the greatest uneasiness, was, that he could by no persuasions be induced to take a wife; and, consequently, they feared that the noble line in which they took so great a pride, should become extinct in case of his death, and that the government, under which they had ever lived in great felicity, might pass into the hands of a stranger: they therefore petitioned him to take the matter into his consideration; and that for the good of his people, he would allow them to propose for him, or himself select for wife, a lady, the best and gentlest born in all the land.

The Marquis listened to their petition with much kindness of manner, and answered, that although he had never thought to be restricted within the bonds of matrimony, yet, for the welfare and safe government of his people, that he would consent to choose for himself a wife upon the earliest occasion. 'And now,' he concluded, 'I charge you on your lives to assure me, that whoever I may think fit to wed, you will, during her whole life, bear her all honour and worship, both in word and work, as though she were the daughter of an Emperor. And farthermore,' said he, 'this shall ye swear, that ye will never murmur at the choice I may make, from what condition soever of life she may be taken; for since at your requests I consent to forego my liberty, wherever I fix my heart, there shall be my partner for life. Grant me this condition, or I dismiss the matter altogether.' They heartily made oath to abide by his decree, and departed, beseeching him to appoint an early day for his nuptials, which request, to their great satisfaction, he granted, and fixed a certain day for the ceremony: at the same time he gave orders to the officers of his household to make full preparation in honour of the solemnity.

Not far from the palace of the Marquis stood a village, pleasantly situated, which supplied ample provision both for the inhabitants and cattle in its neighbourhood. Among the poor folk of this village lived one, named Janicola, who was accounted the poorest of them all, and he had a fair daughter, called Griselda. Fair she was to behold; but if I were to speak of virtuous beauty, then was she the fairest under the sun. Poorly and humbly brought up, her wants were all of the simplest nature. Simple was her diet, and constantly laborious was her life. Yet, though this young creature was of a tender age, within her virgin breast was enclosed a grave and mature spirit. Her poor old father she cherished with great love and reverence; she tended his sheep in the field, and her only hours of idleness were her hours of sleep.

The Marquis, as he rode out hunting, had frequently fixed his eyes upon Griselda; not in an idle or wanton humour, but with a grave and musing look; commending in his heart her womanly air and modest demeanour, her goodness and dutiful conduct as a daughter:

and he thought that if ever he should wed at all, he would marry her only.

The wedding day had arrived, and no one could guess who was destined to be the bride; which made his subjects conclude that their Lord was still beguiling them. Notwithstanding their doubts and surmises, however, he had given orders, on Griselda's account, for various ornaments and jewels, set in gold and azure, such as rings and brooches meet for a bridal array. And for her clothing, measure was taken of a young maiden most resembling her in height and shape. Towards noon of the wedding-day, when the chambers of the palace and the bridal feast were all prepared, the Marquis, in rich apparel, with all the lords and ladies in his company who were invited to the feast, and all his retinue of knights, attended by musicians, playing sweet melodies, took his way to the village I have described.

Griselda, perfectly innocent—heaven knows —of the thought that all this display was prepared for her, had been to a well for water, and was returning home as quickly as she could, in order that she might have sight of the ceremony, and of the expected and unknown Marchioness. So while she was standing on the threshold of her own door, surrounded by her village companions, the Marquis drew near and called her out by name. Immediately she set down her water-pot in an ox's stall close by the threshold, and on her knees before the Lord, with a sober and steady look, waited his command.

The Marquis, in a sedate and thoughtful tone, asked where her father was. 'My Lord,' said she, 'he is ready here to do your will:' and, without farther delay, she led him forth. Then, taking this poor man aside by the hand, he said: 'Janicola! I can no longer conceal the pleasant wish of my heart: if you consent, I will, before I leave this place, take your daughter for my wife until my life's end. As my faithful liegeman, I know your attachment and love for me; say then, do you accept my proposal to become your son-in-law?'

The suddenness of this appeal so amazed poor Janicola, that, blushing with confusion and abashment, he stood trembling in the presence of his liege Lord; and all he could answer was: 'My true and dear Lord! I have no will in this matter—order according to your own will and pleasure.'—'Then,' said the Marquis in a low and mild voice, 'I wish to have a conference with you both within doors; for I would know from her own mouth, and before you, her father, whether it be her free will to become my wife, and subject to my dominion. All this shall be done in your presence; and no word will I say to her out of your hearing.' While the three were arranging the conditions within, the neighbours flocked about the house, talking together of the dutiful and loving behaviour of Griselda towards her father, and of her honest and simple bearing to all, while she, unaccustomed to the presence of such a guest, and in such a place, stood pale and wondering at the event. To end the affair, however, as shortly as possible, the Marquis turned to this gentle and very faithful creature, and said: 'Griselda, it pleases your father and myself that I should take you to be my wife; and I think you will not reject our wishes. Yet, since our union must be concluded hastily, bethink yourself whether you

THE CLERK'S TALE.

'The Marquis turned to this gentle and very faithful creature, and said: "Griselda, it pleases your father and myself that I should take you to be my wife; and I think you will not reject our wishes."'

can assent to the following questions which I would first ask of you. Are you prepared with a good heart to yield yourself to my will and pleasure, whether it bring you joy or sorrow? Will you, without grudge, either by word or look, gainsay the least or greatest of my commands? Pledge me this, and here I confirm our alliance.'

Wondering at all this, and trembling with fear and anxiety, she said, 'My Lord! unworthy as I am of the high honour you intend me, I here declare—loth as I am to die—that I will endure that extremity rather than disobey you willingly either in thought or deed.' 'This is enough,' said he; 'then are you my own Griselda;' and leading her forth to the people, he proclaimed her to them as his wife, desiring all who were attached to his own person and family to honour, love, and obey her. And as it was his wish that she should not appear at the palace in her mean attire, he ordered some of the women in his retinue to assist in spoiling her of those peasant's weeds, a task the ladies were not blithe to execute, as somewhat disdaining to handle her lowly gear;

notwithstanding, however, this fresh and lovely maiden came forth from their hands, from head to foot, both in mind and body worthy of her strange advancement. With their courtly and delicate fingers they tressed up her rudely flowing hair, binding it with a richly-jewelled crown, and all her robes and dresses were studded and knit together with precious stones and ornaments of gold, so that the people scarcely knew their poor companion in her splendid transformation.

The Marquis confirmed his pledge upon the spot by placing on her finger the bridal ring, and forward they paced to the palace; she being mounted upon a snow-white palfrey, the joyful populace following and welcoming; while some held her horse's bridle, others looked upon her face to see how she sustained her sudden honours:—and so the day was passed in gladness, feasting, and revelry.

I would not willingly delay the current of my story; but it is to my purpose here to tell you, that so bountifully had heaven showered its grace and favour upon this new Marchioness, that so far from betraying the lowliness of her birth, her discreet deportment would have honoured the daughter of an Emperor. They who had known her from her infancy could scarcely bring their minds to conceive that she was the homely child of old Janicola; and though she was in her former condition ever virtuous and kind, yet so had her excellent qualities increased, so full of bounty, so discreet, and sweet of speech, so courteous, and worthy of reverence, and so ready to embrace the hearts of all, that no one could look upon her face and not love her. The fame of her high bounty had spread so far and wide, that all ranks, young and old, went to Saluzzo only to behold her.

Thus, Walter, not lowly, but royally wedded, lived in peace and honour; and because he had the sense to discern honest virtue in a mean estate, he enjoyed the rare credit of being esteemed by all a prudent man. Not only, however, was the understanding of Griselda equal to every wifely accomplishment, but when the case required it, she could dispose herself for the common benefit. During her husband's absence, every rancour and discord among the people she would with her sagacity, and placid demeanour and persuasiveness, smooth into peace and goodwill. So wise and ripe was her discourse, and her judgment so equitable, that the people would say, she was sent from heaven to redress the wrongs of mankind.

To the great joy of all, in due time Griselda presented her husband with a daughter.

During the suckling of this babe, it entered the mind of the Marquis to put his wife upon some severe trials that he might prove her steadfastness of heart :—a needless course, however some may praise its subtleness of purpose, for he had already assayed, and found her ever good and true :—evil, therefore, must be the thought, that, without cause, could put a wife to the anguish of trial. Nevertheless, he acted as you shall hear. One night, as she lay in bed, he approached her with a stern and troubled face, and said: 'I presume, Griselda, you have not forgotten the day on which I took you from your humble plight, and raised you to the highest rank of nobility—I say, you have not lost sight of your former humbleness of condition; take heed, then, of what I am now about to say to you. You are yourself aware how, not long ago, you entered this palace; and though to my heart you have been ever dear, yet are you not acceptable to my nobles, who chafe at and grudge their becoming subject to one of your low origin; and these heart-burnings have increased since the birth of your child. Since, therefore, it has ever been my care to live at peace with my people, I cannot in the present case be regardless of that duty, but must dispose of your child, not as I would, but as my nobles please. Greatly, heaven knows, as I abhor this course, yet I would do nothing without your knowledge; although, at the same time, I require the performance of your marriage vow, that on this occasion you show the patience of your spirit by yielding yourself to my will.'

When she had heard this dreadful speech, with a steady voice and unshaken aspect, she said, 'My Lord! my child and I, with full obedience on my part, are all your own—you may cherish or abandon your own property. And, as the good God shall protect me, I declare that no creature wearing your form can ever distress or change my heart. I desire nothing, and I dread to lose nothing, yourself alone excepted; this thought is rooted in my heart, and it shall ever remain so: neither length of time nor death itself can deface or change the courage of my purpose.'

The Marquis secretly rejoiced at her answer, but he feigned otherwise; and leaving the chamber with a sorrowful air, he privately conferred with a dependant, whom he possessed of his intention, and sent to the apartment of his wife. This commoner was a sort of sergeant, who had heretofore been found trustworthy in important matters—such agents, we know, can also at times be equally faithful in a cruel errand. The Lord well knew that he both loved and feared him; so when the fellow had received his orders, he silently stalked into the room.

'Madam,' said he, 'it is not for one like me to inform you of our hard necessity to obey in all things the will of our Lords; and you must forgive me, who am constrained to do that which of my own free will I would refuse. I am commanded to take away this child.' He said no more, but roughly seizing the babe, behaved as though he would have slain it before its mother's face. Griselda, who was doomed to endure all, and to consent to all, sat still and meek as a lamb, and let the cruel sergeant pursue his course. At length, however, she gently entreated the man (as though he had been one of noble birth) that she might kiss her child before it died: and so, with woful face, she laid its little body in her lap; and lulling it, and kissing it, and with a mother's heart yearning for the blessing of its safety, she said with her soft and benign voice—'Farewell, my child! I shall behold you no more. To that Father, with whose cross I have marked you, do I commend your sinless soul.' Then, turning to the sergeant, she meekly said, 'Now take your infant charge, and follow my Lord's commands;—but oh! if they be for death, one thing I entreat at your hands, that you would bury its little body beyond the violation of beasts and carrion fowl:' so constant was this mother in her adversity. The man returned no answer to her petition, but, taking up the child, went back to his Lord, and told him all he had heard and seen; who, indeed, began to repent his sternness; but, with the wilful steadiness of one who had never known control, he persisted in his cruel purpose; and ordered the sergeant, upon pain of death, not to disclose the least circumstance of the affair, but carefully to take the infant to his sister, the Countess di Panico, at that time living in Bologna, beseeching her to foster it with every regard to the gentleness of its birth; bidding her also, whatever might happen, to conceal from every one the name of its parents. The sergeant departed to fulfil his errand: and now we will return to the Marquis, who was busily curious to discover whether in word or demeanour any change were wrought in his wife; but he still found her the same kind and staid Griselda; as humble, as ready both in love and duty was she in all respects; nor did she even speak of her child. From that dreadful day no accident or sting of adversity could bring the name of her daughter to pass her lips.

Four years had now elapsed when Griselda gladdened the heart of her husband, and fulfilled the wishes of his people, by giving them an heir to the Marquisate. All went on prosperously, the child increased in strength and beauty of form; it was the delight of its parents, and the pride of its future subjects; all seemed satisfied—all happy. All *seemed*, but all were not happy; for at the age of two years, when the nurse's duty had ceased, and that this tender seedling had begun to shoot its little roots deeply, and more and more firmly every day to twine about the heart of its mother, the demon of temptation and mistrust again possessed the mind of that wilful and unrelenting husband. How hardly can men restrain the wantonness of power when a patient creature is subjected to its control!

'Griselda!' said he, 'I have already made known to you that the people look with an evil eye upon our marriage; and since the birth of my son this discontent has increased. The constant talk now is,—'When the reigning Marquis dies, we shall have the blood of the pauper Janicola to be our Lord, and to rule over us.' These murmurs, as you may suppose, cut me to the heart: I cannot but see their dissatisfaction; and though I do not hear, I am made to know the cause of their offence. As, therefore, it is the desire of my heart to reign in peace, I have resolved to remove my son and dispose of him as I formerly did of his sister; of which determination I give you warning, in order that you may be prepared for the event, and not give way to any sudden grief, but endure all my decrees with your promised patience and steadfastness.'

'I have said,' she replied, 'and I will never repeal my oath, that nothing which you may command will I gainsay. Though my children be both slain, you are my Lord and their Lord, and may do with your own as you list: their mother has had no part in their lot, but pain in the first instance, and unavailing sorrow ever after. As when I first left my home to come to you, I left my all, even to my clothing; so I then left my will and my liberty when I put on your array. Follow, therefore, the inclination of your heart. If I had the prescience to know that my death would give you ease, of a surety would I die forthwith—Death can bear no comparison with my love.'

When he beheld the patience of his wife, he cast down his eyes, wondering at her constancy, yet glad at heart: with a show of sorrow, however, in his countenance, he left the room. His place was supplied by the same ill-looking minion that had performed his master's former hateful errand; who seized her lovely child and bore it away amid the blessings and embraces of its mother; yet carrying it tenderly, as he did its sister, to the Countess at Bologna.

It is not to be supposed that these acts on the part of the Marquis were executed in so secret a corner but that the vileness of their odour bewrayed itself. The slander against him had begun to spread far and wide, that, wickedly, and with a cruel heart, he had first taken to wife a woman in poverty, and had afterwards privately murdered her children. He then, who had been the idol of his people, now became the object of their abhorrence. Notwithstanding all which fearful rumour (and the stigma of murderer is the heaviest load that can be thrown upon a man's conscience), such was the cruelty of his purpose, and the determination of his obstinacy, that he would not relax a jot from pursuing to its utmost extent the plan he had formed for proving the faithfulness of this gentle and already too mild-conditioned woman.

When his daughter had reached the age of twelve years, he privately commissioned the same messenger to draw up papers, counterfeiting a Bull from the Pope at Rome, sanctioning a dissolution of the bonds of marriage between himself and Griselda, upon the plea that it had been the cause of rancour and dissension between the people and him, their ruler. The rude commonalty, who are seldom slow to be deceived, gave ear to the proclamation, and (no wonder) thought it was all true. But when the tidings were brought to Griselda, she was smitten to the heart with the new and unlooked for cruelty of the blow; yet, like a lamb, she abided in dumb anguish the bitterness of this unpitying storm, nor ever once let a word of upbraiding fall from her lips.

To draw as shortly as possible to the conclusion of my tale, the Marquis secretly sent a letter to his brother-in-law, the Count di Panico, requesting him to bring home again, openly, and with all the pomp due to their estate, both the children that had been placed under his protection; but on no account to disclose any other circumstance respecting them, than that the maiden was destined to become the new bride of the Marquis di Saluzzo.[1] The Count strictly fulfilled his brother's commission, and, upon a day appointed, set forth towards Saluzzo with his young charge and her brother, at that time only seven years of age; the former gorgeously arrayed, and attended by a numerous and honourable retinue.

Notwithstanding all this wicked usage, the Marquis determined still farther to prove utterly the courage and forbearance of his wife. I need not ask the women whether she had not given him sufficient proof of a virtuous love and steady devotion; but you will bear in mind that in the opening of my story I told you, when describing the faults in his character, 'that he was too prone to gratify the desires of the present moment, without regard to the

---

[1] The young reader is doubtless aware that in Italy females are disposed in marriage at an age when in this country they would scarcely have quitted the nursery.

future;' add to which, that he was as firm in fulfilling the object of those desires, as she was patient and constant in her oath of obedience. Consequently, upon a certain day, in the open audience of his whole Court, he delivered to her, in a stern and boisterous tone, the following declaration.

'Although I acknowledge, Griselda, the great comfort I have experienced in your truth, goodness, and obedience, since we have been husband and wife (though not in the quality of your lineage, or in the wealth I took with you), yet now I find, of a sad truth, that loftiness of birth and dignity of station are burthened with a heavy and dreary servitude. I may not act like the meanest hind in my domains; but all my people, strengthened by this order from the Pope, daily require of me to take another wife; to which constraint I have so far yielded, that it has become necessary to inform you that my new bride, your successor, is now on her road to Saluzzo. Be therefore strong of heart, and void her place. All the dowry you brought me, I give back again —prosperity never flows in an unbroken current; return, therefore, to your father's house, and strive to bear with an even heart this stroke of fortune.'

She answered him in a tone of patience that was a marvel to the whole assembly:—'My Lord, I know, and have always felt, that no comparison can be drawn between my poverty and your magnificence. At no time did I ever esteem myself higher in degree of worth than to be your chamber-woman: and in this palace, of which you exalted me to be the lady, I take heaven to witness, and am now glad I did so, that I never considered myself the mistress of it, but the dutiful minister to your worthiness: and this, above every other earthly creature, I shall ever continue to be. That in your graciousness you so long retained me in a state of honour and nobility, of which I was unworthy, I thank both God and you, and hope he may bountifully repay it you. I willingly return to my father, and with him will end my days. In that cot was I fostered from my tenderest childhood; there will I pass the remainder of my life—a widow, clean in her conduct, and with an unupbraiding heart. And since I gave to you all I could give, and came a spotless maiden, and am your true wife, heaven forbid that the wife of such a Lord should be united to another husband. As regards your new bride, I pray for your happiness and prosperity: I freely yield her that place where I was wont to be so blessed: for since it is your pleasure, my Lord (who wert formerly the home in which my heart had nestled), that I should depart, I am ready to go when you command. But when you offer to restore such dowry as I first brought, too well do I bear in mind that it was my wretched clothes—Oh! good God! how gentle and kind you seemed by your speech and your countenance on the day of our marriage! True it is, and I find it so, for in myself I have proved the effect, that love when old is not the same as love when it is young. Yet, be sure, my Lord, that for no adversity, even were it to die upon this occasion, shall it ever be, that either in word or deed, I repent of having given you my whole heart, freely, and without reserve.

'My Lord, you know that in my father's hut you stripped me of my lowly weeds, and clad me in an array suitable to my altered fortune: to you I brought nothing but faith, and nakedness, and a maidenly purity:—here again I restore your clothing, and your wedding-ring —for ever. The remnant of your jewels are in your chamber. Naked I came from my father's house, and naked must I return. Yet I would hope that it is not your intention to send me forth utterly destitute: you could not do so dishonest a thing as to expose her who had borne your children to the stare of the ruthless multitude—let me not like a worm go by the way—remember, however unworthy, I *was* your wife. Therefore, in return for that unspotted chastity—the only dowry I could bring to you—vouchsafe to me the simple under garment I was wont to wear. And now, my Lord, I take my leave.'

'The under-coat,' said he, 'which is now upon your back, you may take away with you:' but scarcely had he spoken the words than he left the place, for he could not look upon her for compassion. In the presence of the Court she stripped herself of her noble robes, and in her under-dress, bare-headed and bare-footed, set forward towards her father's house: the people following, weeping, and cursing fortune as they went along: while she maintained her womanly courage, and with dry eyes never once uttered a word. Her father, who heard the tidings of her usage, bitterly lamented the day of his birth. For this poor old man had ever mistrusted their marriage; suspecting, from the first, that when the Lord was weary of his fancy, he would begin to think it a disparagement to his estate to have stooped so low, and would dismiss her upon the first occasion. He went out hastily to meet her, for he knew by the coil of the populace that she was coming, and covered her with her peasant's dress, the tears all the while streaming down his old face.

Thus dwelt for some time with her father this flower of wifely patience; who neither by word or look, before the people, gave notice of the offence she had received, or any token that she remembered her former high estate; and no wonder, for even then she was ever humble. She affected no delicacy or tenderness of person—no pomp—no show of royalty;

but was full of patient kindness; discreet and honourable; and meek and constant to her husband. Our writers have praised Job above all men for his humility; but though they have said little in behalf of women for the steadiness of their truth, no man can acquit himself in humility like a woman; or show half a woman's constancy.

The Count di Panico having set out from Bologna, the report was spread abroad that he was bringing with him a new Marchioness in such pomp and splendour as had never been seen before in all West Lombardy. Before the arrival of the Count, the Marquis sent for poor Griselda; who, with that never-failing cheerfulness of countenance which sprang from the excess of her love, and because she should again see his face, and not from any swollen, selfish thought of a favourable change in her condition, instantly obeyed his summons, and on her knees greeted him with reverence and discretion.

'Griselda,' said he, 'it is my will and pleasure that the lady, whom I am about to marry, should be received to-morrow at my palace with every distinction of royalty; and therefore would I have each attendant, according to his office and rank, perfect in the fulfilment of his duty. As I have no female so well acquainted as yourself with my taste and fancy in the arranging of my apartments (for you have long been accustomed to consult my pleasure in that respect), I have sent for you to superintend this part of the general preparation. And though the fashion and quality of your dress is unsuited to the sphere of a Court, that may be excused, since it will not interfere with the performance of that duty which I know you will use for my satisfaction.'

'Not only my Lord,' said she, 'am I free and willing to perform your commands; but it is the desire of my heart to serve and please you without fainting and without repinement. Neither in weal nor woe shall I ever cease to love you with the truest intention, above the whole world.' And with that word she set about her task of ordering, superintending, and arranging the suites of rooms.

About noon the Count, with the two children,

arrived before the palace gate, the populace crowding round to see the cavalcade, and the rich quality of all the furniture; the greater part of them talking among themselves in praise of the Marquis's wisdom in changing his wife; 'for not only,' said they, 'is this new one younger and more beautiful than Griselda, but she is of gentle birth, and her offspring will be more agreeable to us.' Then the handsome face of her little brother delighted them;—and, to crown all, they, who shortly before traduced him as a murderer, were now unanimous in applauding his government. Thus has it ever been with you, misjudging multitude! unstable as the veering vane! indiscreet, unfaithful!—ever seeking something new. Your applause is purchased dearly enough at the price of a mite: your judgment is false and hollow; and your constancy a rope of sand. Fool, indeed, is he who places confidence in you. So it was with the poor gazing creatures of Saluzzo; the novelty of having another Marchioness —no matter the price of injustice at which she was purchased — changed at once their discontent to satisfaction. But I will turn to a pleasanter subject—the zeal and constancy of Griselda.

Active in everything that could tend to forward the entertainment, she was the wonder and astonishment of all the household, who shortly before had received her commands as a mistress, yet delivered in the same mild and even tone. And when the guests arrived, she was seen in her peasant's dress, receiving each, according to their station, with a simple dignity and discretion which surprised them all, when they considered her poor appointment, ignorant as they were of her former quality. Nor did she even refrain from praising the beauty of the young maiden and her brother. At length, when the company had sat down to the feast, the Marquis sent for her, and in a sporting tone enquired how she approved of the beauty of his new wife.—'My Lord,' said she, 'I never beheld a fairer lady;—happiness and prosperity attend you both to the end of your lives. One thing allow me, I beseech you; which is, to warn you against tormenting this tender maiden, as it has been your will to distress me; for she has been softly fostered, and cannot undergo the trials of adversity like one who, in early life, had striven with poverty and rude labour.'

At length, when Walter found that her patient and untroubled spirit triumphed over every offence that could be offered to her, and that she remained firm in her innocence, and unshaken as a wall, his sturdy heart began to melt, in thinking of all her wifely steadfastness; and breaking forth into a passionate strain of admiration—'Enough! enough! my own Griselda,' said he, 'no longer shall you be terrified with violence and unkindness: I have tried your faith and benignity, as never woman was tried, both in high estate and in poverty. Now do I, indeed, know that you are truth itself.' And then he caught her in his arms, and kissed her very affectionately; while the gentle creature herself appeared like one suddenly aroused from sleep; she regarded not his caresses; she heard nothing of his speech; and when her senses had somewhat recovered, he said to her—'Griselda! by the great and good God, who suffered for our transgressions, you are still my wife—I have no other—have had no other, and shall have no other. This maiden whom you supposed to be my wife is your daughter, and this, her brother, shall inherit my kingdom. Truly and lawfully did you bear them to me; and all this time have I kept them privately with my sister, at Bologna. Take them again, and be assured you have not been unnaturally bereft of your offspring. And now, let those who have deemed otherwise of my conduct be informed, that with no malice or wilful cruelty have I acted as I did, but to make trial of your womanly virtue—not to murder your children—Heaven forbid! but to secrete them till I knew the temper of your heart.'

When she had heard this speech, the great flood of joy that burst upon her amazed senses, together with the suddenness of the change, so wrought upon her tender frame, that she swooned at his feet. And when she recovered, she called her children to her, and taking them in her arms, piteously weeping, she embraced them over and over again, tenderly kissing them with those motherly lips; and all the while the tears streamed over their hair and faces.—Oh! it was an affecting thing to have seen her helpless insensibility, and then to hear again her meek and cordial voice!

'Gramercy, my good Lord and husband! may God repay thee with thanks, that thou hast spared to me our dear children. Seeing that I thus stand in thy gracious favour, I feel that I could joyfully give up my life; and if it be God's will, never at a more blissful season than when I know that they, for whom I sorrowed, have been saved from an early grave.

'Oh my dear young children; your woful mother had no other thought than that you had been left a prey to some foul vermin'—and with those words her senses failed again; yet, all the while, she held them so closely in her embrace, that they were separated only by force: while those who stood around wept many a tear for pity. At length the voice of her husband and the subsiding of her sorrow restored her, and she arose, abashed at having exposed the feebleness of her nature. All strove to divert her thoughts by little courtesies and speeches of kindness, till she regained her benign and cheerful countenance. Walter, too, let slip no occasion of redeeming all his sternness and deeds of cruelty, by pleasant looks and cherishings; and as she was so sweet a creature to behold in her hours of adversity and trial, you may suppose how fair a sight was her face of content and happiness.

After a time the ladies in attendance conducted her to her former chamber, where they stripped off (and for ever) the peasant's garb, and having arrayed her in a robe of cloth-of-gold, and set upon her head a jewelled crown, she returned to the hall amid the honours and congratulations of the assembly. Such was the joyous termination of this painful day: and the revelry was kept up till the stars shone at their brightest; and the feast was more costly and magnificent than that given upon their marriage.

And so these two lived many years in prosperity and unbroken concord. The daughter was married to a Lord, of the greatest worth in all Italy; and poor Janicola was furnished with an asylum at Court, where he lived near his daughter in peace and honour, till his spirit gently crept from his body, and returned to Him who gave it. The son succeeded to a peaceful government after his father had left his place. He was fortunate in his marriage, although he did not prove his wife in imitation of his father. The people of this world are not so strong as they were in days of yore; and my author makes this apology for his tale. 'This story,' he says, 'is not intended as a recommendation that wives should imitate Griselda in the plenitude of her humility (for that were utterly impossible), but that everyone should in his degree strive to be patient under reverses and sharp strokes of fortune: for as a woman was so patient to a mortal man, how much more steadfastly should we endure the trials that God may please to inflict upon us. He daily proves our constancy; and his government, however it may appear at the moment, ultimately tends to our advantage. Let us all, then, live in virtuous sufferance.

THE SQUIRE'S TALE:

THE STORY OF CAMBUSCAN.

Our host now called upon the young Squire for his tale, who with great goodwill began the following.

At Sarra, in the land of Tartary, there dwelt a King who had often waged war upon the country of Russia. He was called Cambuscan, and had gained so famous a name for all noble and knightly deeds, that no one in those days could compare with him in renown. He seemed to lack no grace that makes royalty honourable. He was a strict observer of the laws he had sworn to protect; add to which, he was brave, wise, just, and compassionate; true to his word, courteous, young, fresh, and strong, and eager in arms as any bachelor of his court. To crown all, he was fair of person, fortunate in all his adventures, and maintained so sumptuous a display of regalities that there was not such another King in all the East.

This imperial Tartar had by his wife Elfeta two sons; the one was named Camballo, and the other Algarsife. He had also a daughter, the youngest of the three, who was called Canace. My sober English, and more sober fancy, are unequal to the description of her rare beauty. No one could come worthily to such a task, unless it were an orator, fully provided with the gay colours of his rhetoric: but as I lack the eloquence due to such a theme, you must be content to know that she was esteemed the fairest maiden in her father's dominions.

It was the custom with Cambuscan to give a feast on the day of his nativity every year; and on the twentieth of his reign he made a proclamation through all his city of Sarra, that it would be observed with unwonted solemnity and splendour. The sun was in the young and lusty spring of the year, when the weather is bright and shining; when the birds and every creature feel the coming forth of the tender green, and all pour out their love and gladness, as it were, both for the warm days, and their protection against the cold and keen sword of winter.

When the day arrived, Cambuscan, in his royal robes and diadem, and seated aloft in the banquetting hall of his palace, presented to the nobles of the land so rich and solemn an entertainment, that the like was never seen before. It would occupy a summer's day to describe to you all the array of the various services—the number and appointment of the sewers and seneschals; the rare daintiness of the meats, and sum of the dishes; the silver and the gold, the spices, the wine, and the odour steaming from lofty censers. I therefore pass them with no farther notice, and follow the stream of my history.

It happened that after the third course, while the King was hearkening to his minstrels playing delicious melodies before him at his board, suddenly there rode in at the hall door a Knight upon a horse of brass, holding in his hand a fair and broad mirror. Upon his thumb he wore a golden ring, and at his side hung a naked sword. In this fashion he rode straight towards the upper table. Throughout the hall not a word was spoken for astonishment at this Knight; and every eye was fixed upon him.

This sudden stranger, who was richly armed, save that his head was bare, saluted the King and Queen with all their nobles according to their degrees, with so high a reverence and dignity in speech and demeanour, that had old Gawain returned from fairy-land, he could not have amended his courtesy by the alteration of a single word. Having fulfilled the ceremony of introduction with a sweet, yet manly voice, he addressed himself to the high board after the manner following:—' The King of Arabia and of India, my liege Lord, offers to you his salutation upon the event of this solemn day; and in honour of your feast, he hath sent you, by me, (who am, at command, your dutiful servant,) this horse of brass, which possesses the power of conveying you to whatever quarter of the earth you may please to ride, the within compass of a day. Or, if you desire to soar like an eagle, it will evermore bear you without danger through the region of birds, to the place of your destination; and by the turning of a little pin, will convey you home again. So staid and soft is it in progress, that you may, without fear, sleep upon its back. The artist who accomplished this wondrous mechanism had wrought many an engine of miraculous power, and the finishing of this, his last work, engaged him during the revolving of many cycles of years.

'The mirror which I hold in my hand possesses the power to make known to you any approaching calamity, either to your own person or your kingdom; it will also discover who are your friends, and who your foes; and, above all, if any fair lady have disposed of her heart to a Knight, and he be secretly unfaithful, this mirror will lay open all his treason, however subtlely he may wear it concealed. This, with the ring of gold, my royal master hath sent in honour of this occasion to your most excellent and right worshipful daughter here—the Lady Canace.

'The virtue of the ring is this;—if my

Lady please to wear it on her thumb, or in her purse, she will immediately comprehend the language of every bird that flies, and have the power of answering it again in its native tongue. Also, it will give her the knowledge of all herbs, with their virtues, for the cure of wounds, be they ever so severe.

'The naked sword, hanging by my side, is of such a temper, that whomsoever it may strike it will cleave his armour, although it were thick as the knotted oak. And he that is wounded with the blow, will never be whole again, until, of your grace, you please to stroke the smitten part with its flat side; when it will straight close again and heal. This virtue will never fail so long as the sword shall remain in your grasp.'

When the Knight had fulfilled his commission, he rode out of the hall and alighted. His horse, which dazzled like the unclouded sun, stood as still as a stone in the centre of the Court. The Knight being conducted to his chamber, was unarmed, and placed according to his degree at the feasting board. The presents—that is to say, the mirror and the sword—were given into the keeping of proper officers, who conveyed them to a high tower in the castle; and the ring was borne with great state to the Lady Canace as she sate at the table. The horse remained in the Court fixed to the earth, and immoveable: no machinery, or any unskilful hand, could stir it from its place, till the Knight showed the hidden manner of removing it,—which will be explained hereafter.

The populace crowded into the Court to see this wonderful horse, murmuring round it like a swarm of bees: and as they examined its figure, each praised its fair proportion—its height, and exact length, and great breadth of chest, all formed for swiftness and endurance—like that large breed of Lombardy; and, withal, it was as quick of eye as a high-blood courser of Apulia—in short, all agreed, that from hoof to head, and from head to tail, neither nature nor art could supply an improvement. But what most raised their wonder was, how it could move, being made of brass. Some said it came from fairy land; others referred to their favourite old poets, and said it was like the winged Pegasus: or that mayhap it was another Grecian horse, which wrought the downfall of Troy. 'My heart,' said one, 'misgives me—I doubt that there are armed men within, who at a given signal will steal out and surprise our city by stratagem. I consider it proper that the affair should be enquired into.' Another whispered to his neighbour, 'He's quite out there—'tis more like some magical contrivance that jugglers frequently display at these high festivities.' And so they debated and questioned the affair, like all ignorant and common minds, that are ever blythe in imputing a bad motive to inventions which are too subtle for their gross perceptions.

Some were engaged in discourse upon the wonders of the mirror, and how such things could be perceived in it. One among the number made the secret of it appear to the satisfaction of every one, in stating that all might be naturally accomplished by the compositions of angles and acute reflections; and, to display his reading, he said there were many such in Rome; and then referred to Alhazen,

Vitellion, and Aristotle, who have written upon curious mirrors and perspectives.

Others again wondered upon the sword, which was said to pierce through every thing; and turned their conversation upon the renowned King Telephus, and the marvellous spear of Achilles, that could both wound and heal, as with the one of which you now have heard. They discoursed also of the tempering of metal, how it was best hardened, and of the medicines and ingredients used in the process; of all which I am ignorant.

After this they turned to speak of the Lady Canace's curious ring, saying, that they had never heard of the like, unless it were the ring of Moses or of Solomon, which possessed a similar virtue. And so they continued wondering and jangling till the King arose from the feast. Before him walked the loud minstrelsy, marshalling his way to the presence chamber, and all the while, till he was seated upon his throne, sounding their instruments, —that it was a heaven to hear. When this noble King was seated, he ordered the strange Knight to be brought before him, and bids him lead the dance with the Princess Canace. Now came the revel and the jollity, such as no dull man can devise. Festive and fresh as May, and well practised in love's mysteries must he be who could worthily tell you of all the dances so quaint in their figures; of the blithe countenances; the subtle looks and dissemblings, for fear of the detection of jealous rivals: no one could do honour to such a description but the perfect hand of Sir Launcelot, and, therefore, I pass over all this mirth, and leave them dancing till the supper was arrayed and proclaimed. I need not rehearse the variety of the spices and the wine, or the train of ushers and squires; suffice to say, all were entertained from the highest to the lowest with dainties more than I know of.

After supper the King, surrounded by all his rout of Lords and Ladies, went down into the court to look at this horse of brass; and the King enquired of the Knight as to the qualities of this wondrous courser, and how it was to be governed. When the Knight laid his hand upon the rein, the horse began to trample and caper. 'Sire,' said he, ' no other instruction is required as to the management of the steed, than that when you desire to ride to any place, you turn a pin that is fixed in his ear, and which I will privately explain to you; when you may command him to what place or country soever you choose to ride. And when you wish to stop, you bid him descend and turn another pin, (in this lies all your art,) when, at your will, he will stoop from his flight and remain quiet as a stone in that place, and the whole world will not be able to remove him. Or if you wish him to depart alone, turn the pin again, and he will vanish from the sight of every one, and return at command whether by night or by day.'

When the King had learned from the Knight all that was to be done he was glad at his heart and returned to finish the revelry as before. The bridle was carried to a tower in the palace, and placed amongst the rarest jewelry. The horse vanished, I know not whither, from the sight of all. And so I leave this King Cambuscan with his lords feasting in their jollity till day began to spring.

THE SQUIRE'S TALE.

'A falcon, that, perched upon a withered tree, "as white as chalk," was bewailing, with "a voice so piteous that all the wood resounded with her cry," the cruelty and falsehood of her mate, who had ill requited her love and fidelity by deserting her.'

The second part of this story opens with an account of the young Princess Canace rising early on the following morning, the appearance of which is described in Chaucer's own simple and agreeable manner:—'The vapour (says he) that glided up from the earth made the sun look broad and ruddy; nevertheless it was so fair a sight that it inspired her with cheerfulness of heart, as well as on account of the season of the year, the early hour of the morning, and the song of the birds, whose language by means of her magic ring, she was enabled to understand.' The narrative goes on to describe at great length a dialogue she held with a falcon, that, perched upon a withered tree, 'as white as chalk,' was bewailing with 'a voice so piteous that all the wood resounded with her cry,' the cruelty and falsehood of her mate, who had ill requited her love and fidelity by deserting her. If the whole of this portion of the story were transposed into prose, it would, I fear, prove uninteresting to the young reader. The original is clothed in nervous and beautiful verse, and will, at some future period, amply reward the youthful, imaginative mind that has overcome the not arduous toil of comprehending freely the quaint and, unfortunately, obsolete dialect of this very great and beautiful poet.

After informing us that Canace, in pity of the sorrow of her new acquaintance, takes her home, and keeps her in a beautiful mew (or cage) at her own bed's head; 'here,' says the narrator, 'I leave Canace tending her gentle falcon; and, for the present, shall say no more about the ring, till my purpose suit to inform you how the bird regained her repenting lover through the mediation of Camballo, the King's son. Henceforth my purpose is to speak of adventures and battles so marvellous as never before were heard.

'First, I will tell you of Cambuscan, who in his time had won many a fair city; and afterward of Algarsife, how he gained Theodora as his bride; for whose sake he was oft in sharp perils, and was redeemed by the horse of brass: and then of Camballo, who fought in lists with the two brethren for Canace before he could obtain her as his prize.'[1] So, where I

[1] There appears here some mistake either in the original

left off I will begin again the course of my tale.'———And this hopeful promise the poet never fulfilled. The tale of the young Squire remains to be told—and who will dare undertake the task, when even Milton himself would not venture, but says:

> 'Call up him that left half told
> The story of Cambuscan bold;
> Of Cambal and of Algarsife,
> And who had Canace to wife
> That own'd the virtuous ring of glass;
> And of the wondrous horse of brass,
> On which the Tartar King did ride?'

In Book iv. of 'the Faery Queen,' Cantos ii. and iii., Spenser has endeavoured partially to fulfil the task, incompleted by Chaucer. The young reader may feel interested in seeing how one renowned poet would follow in the track of a revered predecessor; I will therefore give a short account of Spenser's continuation of the story.

With that noble modesty that is ever in-

MS. as to the name mentioned, or Chaucer forgot that he had already described Camballo as the *brother* of Canace. How then could he fight 'the two brethren?' and which two, he being one of *the* two, and only two named? and how could he win her to wife?

separable from great minds, he begins by a fine compliment to the genius of his illustrious predecessor, whose poetry he calls, 'a well (or spring) of English undefiled,

'On fame's eternal bead-roll worthy to be filed.'

'But wicked time,' says he, 'that all good thoughts doth waste, and wears out the works of noblest wits, has quite defaced that noble monument; how then may these my rude rhymes hope to endure!' And then he concludes with the following beautiful apostrophe: 'Pardon, therefore, O most sacred, happy spirit! that I thus strive to restore thy lost labours, and rob thee of the reward due to thy great merit—an act no one dared attempt whilst thou wert living, and, being dead, many strive to do in vain; and, but for the infusion of thy own sweet spirit in me, I should, with the like fruitless endeavour, hope to accomplish: and so I follow the footing of thy feet, hoping that I may at last reach thy fair design.' And now to the conclusion (such as it is) of our story.

The beautiful Princess Canace was greatly

beloved by many Lords and Knights, who, from her prudence and tardiness in selecting the hand that she deemed the most worthy to give to her all her worldly comfort, were often times moved to envy and bickerings, great quarrels, and bloody strifes; which her brother, Camballo, perceiving, who was a stout and wise Knight, and fearing the peril which might arise from an increase of such contentions, determined, both for her honour and his own, to end the contest in the following manner.

One day, when the whole troop of warlike wooers were assembled, for the purpose of knowing who should be the chosen husband of the Princess, he decreed that they should select from among the company those three, who, by general consent, were esteemed the hardiest and most valiant knights: that these three should combat with him, and the victor be rewarded with the hand of his sister Canace.

The challenge was a bold one, and Camballo was a bold Knight; but his sister's skill and forethought had given him confidence, for she sent him the wondrous ring which possessed the power to staunch the bleeding of all mortal wounds. The great virtue of that ring was known to all, so that the dread of its redoubted might so appalled that youthful rout, that none of them dared undertake the fight. The delight of love they deemed a wiser course to take, than to hazard life for a fair lady's look. Yet amongst the company were three brethren, all born of one mother, and at one birth; her name was Agape, and their names were Priamond, Diamond, and Triamond. They were all three men of exceedingly great might, and well skilled in the knightly accomplishments of arms. Their mother was a fairy, and possessed the skill of secret things, and all the powers of nature, which by her art she could ply to her own purpose. A beautiful woman, too, she was, and of goodly stature when she chose to discover her native form and face; but, as is the custom with fairies, she passed her days in privacy, and in the wildest and most spacious forests. In this savage chamber, and on this rough couch, she bare and nursed the three champions that have been described.

When these had grown into the ripeness of man's estate, and had begun to show signs of love for deeds of arms, and for the rash provoking of perils, her motherly heart began to doubt and fear for their safety: she therefore, being desirous to know the end of all their days, by her wondrous skill and power, sought her way to the dwelling of the three fatal sisters, who in the bottom of the deep abyss sit in darkness, and round about the dreadful distaff, draw out with unwearied fingers the threads of human life. These fearful beings she humbly accosted, desiring to see the threads of her three sons' lives drawn forth, which Clotho, one of the sisterhood, granting, drew out, to her grief and amazement, threads thin as the spider's web, and so short that their ends seemed to come forth at once.

Having learned the decree of the fates, she entreated, and obtained her request, that the life of each as it terminated, might pass into the next survivor; so that when two were dead, the life of the third might be trebly enlarged. And so returning home with contented heart, this careful fairy concealed from her sons the knowledge of their destiny, warning them from time to time to be faithful and true to each other, whatever might befall them. And this they truly did all their days. Discord never arose amongst them, which greatly augmented their good fame. And now they joined in love of Canace; upon which ground the great battle grew that is about to be described.

Early on the morning of the day which was to witness the event of this hardy challenge to fight with Camballo for Canace, these warlike champions were all assembled in the field. The lists were enclosed, to bar out the press of the assembled multitude. On one side six judges were seated, who were to decide the deeds of arms; and on the other, fair Canace upon a lofty stage, to witness the fortune of the fray, and to be seen as the worthy reward of him that could win her, with the adventuring of his life. Then Camballo first entered the list with a stately step and undaunted countenance, as if he surely knew the victory to be his own. Immediately after came the three brethren, in brave array and goodly carriage, with gilded escutcheons and broad banners displayed: and three times they lowly bowed to the noble maid, all the while the trumpets and clarions blowing loud notes of defiance: which being done, the challenger came forth all armed to point to confirm his challenge; against whom Sir Priamond, equally prepared and equipped, set forward. A trumpet blew, and both rushed together with dreadful force and furious intent, careless of danger, as if they were reckless of sparing that life which should be shortly quenched.

Sir Priamond was practised and thoroughly skilled in the use of the shield and spear, and Camballo was not behind him in the use of his weapons, so that it was hard to decide who was the superior knight. Many mighty strokes, that seemed to carry death with them, were delivered on both sides, but both were so watchful and well eyed, that they were avoided and passed by harmless. Yet one given by Priamond was so strongly urged home, that it struck through Camballo's shoulder, and made him withdraw his shield. He was sorely grieved at this mischance, yet no drop of blood issued from the wound, but uncommon pain, which exasperated his haughty courage and fell revenge. Pain never daunts the mighty heart, but makes it swell the more. With that he fiercely drove his spear close underneath the shield of Priamond, so that it entered his thigh through the mail, and the blood gushed forth upon the green plain. Priamond could not uplift himself, on account of the bitterness of the wound, but reeled to and fro in great bewilderment. When Camballo perceived him to be off his guard, he drove at him again with double vehemence, so that nothing could stay his weapon, till its mortal point was entrenched in his side; where, being firmly fixed, as he was striving to wrest it forth, the staff broke and left the head behind. Then drawing his sword he charged him afresh, and with a desperate lunge it pierced through his beaver, and entering his brow, he fell backward with the force of the stroke, his weary spirit quitting its earthly tenement. Yet did it not vanish into air, or flee as others are wont, to the dreary realms of Pluto, but, according to the prayer of his mother, it quickly passed into his brethren, and so lived anew.

When Diamond, the second born, beheld the fate of his brother, grieving at the heavy sight, he rushed forth with a generous feeling of vengeance to resume the battle, as in reversion of his brother's right; and challenging the virgin as his due, his foe was quickly prepared, and the trumpets sounded the charge. With that they fiercely met together, as though each intended to devour his enemy, and with their axes so heavily smote, that neither plate nor mail could resist the storm, but was shivered like rotten wood, whilst through the rifts the blood poured forth, filling the lookers on with ruth and wonder. Many and many a stroke of mortal design were interchanged and warily avoided; till Diamond, disdaining the long delay of fortune, resolved to bring the event, one way or other, to an issue; and so with a mighty sweep he heaved his murderous axe, and aimed a dreadful blow, which, had it fallen as it was intended, the strife would have quickly ceased; but Camballo, being nimbly on his guard, swerved aside, while the other missing his aim, well-nigh fell with the force of his stroke, an advantage not to be lost by the brother of Canace, for before he could recover himself, and get his exposed side under guard again, with the full stretch of all his might, he severed his head clean from his shoulders. The headless trunk stood upright awhile, then fell prone upon the earth. The spirit, which had inhabited it, straight entering into Triamond, filled him with double life and grief; leaping therefore from his place, he rushed forth into the field against Camballo, and fiercely defied him, who, without delay, prepared for the third onset.

Ye may well wonder how that noble Knight, who had been so sorely pressed and wounded, could thus stand on foot, and renew fight after fight. But had ye then seen him advancing, you would have deemed him some new-born champion, so fresh and fierce he seemed. All this arose from the virtue of the magic ring he wore, which not only prevented the shedding of his blood, but renewed his weakened powers, else could he not have matched three mighty champions, who were equal to a host.

Triamond, naught dreading, or desperate of so glorious a victory, sharply assailed him with a storm of blows that rattled like hail; while the fire flashed from his sword fast as spray from a rock. The blows fell so thickly, and with such vengeance, that Camballo was forced to retreat till the heat of his antagonist's fury had somewhat spent itself, which, as soon as he perceived it begin to abate, through waste of breath, he charged anew with might and main. And so the battle wavered to and fro, yet each deemed he should be the victor; until, at length, Sir Triamond stood still, feeble and faint with loss of blood. But Camballo waxed stronger and stronger through the ring's virtue; his blood was not shed, nor were his powers wasted. Through which advantage he rose in his strength, and struck the other so stern a blow, that it passed through the joint of his hauberk into his throat, and he fell down dead in the sight of all;—yet he was not dead, although the living spirit forsook its nest; one soul only left his body, and winged its way from human misery.

Nevertheless, while the people were gazing on, thinking him dead as he appeared, he started up unawares, like one roused from a dream, and again prepared to assail his foe; who, half afraid of so uncouth a sight, stood still holding idly his sword as though he had seen a ghost, till repeated blows roused him into self defence again. From this time, however, he resolved to fight warily, nor follow on so fast, but rather seek to save himself; which Triamond perceiving, thought he began to faint, and that the victory was his own. Therefore he raised his mighty hand, with intent to make an end of all that should withstand the blow, which Camballo watching, was not slow to avoid; and at the same instant, while the other's arm was raised to its height, he struck him from behind his shield full in the arm-pit, so that his sword passed through his body. The dreadful stroke, however, held on its way, and falling heavily upon Camballo's crest, smote him so hugely that it felled him to the earth, and carved a ghastly wound in his head, and indeed had not the sword first rested on the brim of his broad-plated shield, it would have cloven him down to the breast. Thus both fell dead at once, upon the field, each giving his antagonist the victory.

When the multitude saw this event, they surely deemed the war concluded: the judges arose; the marshals of the field broke up the lists; and Canace began to bewail her dearest friend and brother. But, suddenly, both arose again, the one from the swoon in which he had lain, and the other breathing out another spirit, and each commenced a fresh attack. Long did they continue in this manner, as though the battle had only then begun, despising alike strokes, wounds, and weapons; so desirous were they to end the strife, that neither cared to guard or to avoid danger; and so weary were they with fighting, that life itself seemed irksome, and preservation an evil.

Thus while the event hung doubtfully in the balance, and all stood gazing in secret fear of the fatal issue, suddenly they heard far away the noise as of a dangerous tumult, confused with the cries of women and shouts of men. At which the champions stood still a little to learn the meaning of the clamour, when they perceived one in a strangely fashioned car, driving towards them with the fury of a storm. The car was bedecked in a wondrous manner, with gold and many gorgeous ornaments, after the fancy of the old Persian monarchs; and, strange to tell, it was drawn by two grim lions, whose cruel nature was brought under subjection and made to obey the rider's will. And in the car sat a bright and surpassingly fair lady, who seemed one of the company of angels. She was deeply skilled in the subtle arts of magic, having for many a year been well instructed in such lore by the fairy her mother; understanding, therefore, by her power, in how evil a plight her beloved brother, Triamond, at that time stood, she hastened to protect him and pacify the strife which had caused such deadly doings. So, as she passed through the press of people who thronged to gaze upon her, her angry team breaking their peaceful curbs, dashed through the heaps as if they had been folded sheep, rolling them in the dust. Some shrieked with fear, others howled with pain; some laughed, and others shouted for wonder.

This beautiful lady bore in her right hand a wand, about which were twined two serpents crowned with an olive garland. It was like the famous rod that Mercury bears when he goes forth with some charge from the Gods. In her other hand she held a fair cup filled to the brim with nepenthe. Nepenthe is a celestial cordial, ordained by the Gods to assuage all grief of the heart; to chase away bitter contention, and anguish from rage and strife, and to establish instead sweet peace in the troubled mind. Few men but those who are sedate and wise do the Gods permit to taste of nepenthe; such as drink, however, find eternal happiness.

When she had arrived at the side of the lists, she gently struck the rail with her wand, and it flew open to give her entrance. Then, stepping from her car, she gracefully saluted all; first, her brother, whom she tenderly loved, and Camballo next, whose rueful look made her change colour, for she was secretly in love with that princely Knight. They slightly returned her salutation, and instantly prepared to renew the combat. When she saw this, she threw herself down upon the bloody field, and with tears and prayers besought them to be at peace with each other. But, finding that entreaties availed her nothing, she struck them slightly with her powerful wand; when, suddenly, as if their hearts had failed them, the swords fell from their hands, and they remained fixed like men in a trance. So, while their minds were bound by this master spirit, she reached to them the golden cup, of which, being parched with toil and thirst, they drank a hearty draught. And now behold another wonder! No sooner had they tasted the heavenly liquor, than all their bitter enmity was changed into brotherly love. They embraced and plighted hands in eternal friendship. The multitude seeing this sudden change,—the friendly agreement of such mortal foes,—shouted for joy till the heavens rang again.

All this when the gentle Canace beheld, she hastily descended from her lofty seat to know the cause of these strange tidings. And when she saw how that cruel war was ended, and those deadly foes turned into faithful friends, with a lovely demeanour she greeted the lady who had so well wrought that happy change, entertaining her with suitable courtesies, and professions of true friendship and affection.

So, when all was happily accorded, the trumpets sounded, and in great glee the company arose to depart; the champions choosing to march home together, and the wise lady, whose name was Cambina, taking by her side into her car the fair Canace, fresh as a morning rose; and so they went along cheered and admired by the people.

And this fair party spent their days in bands of mutual alliance, for Triamond had Canace to wife, with whom he lived long and happily; and Camballo no less rejoiced in his union with Cambina. So all loved and were beloved alike, and no such lovers have been found since their days.

THE PARDONER'S TALE:

THE STORY OF THE DEATH SLAYERS.

PROLOGUE.

'Now, my good friend, Master Pardoner,' said our host, 'let us have from you a right merry tale of well-conceited jests.'—'It shall be done,' said he, 'by St. Ronion. But, first, let me take a snack of cake, and a draught at this ale-house.' Forthwith all the gentles in the company began to cry, 'No, no, let us have no ribaldry: tell us some moral thing, that we may learn; some sound sense, and we will gladly listen to you.'—'Very well,' said he, 'but give me time to think of an honest tale while I take my liquor. . . . . My Lords and gentlemen,' said he, 'whenever I am about to perform duty in church, my first care is to learn by rote all I have to preach, and then to pitch my voice in a full and high key, ringing it out as round and clear as a bell. My theme is always, and ever has been the same: " Radix malorum est cupiditas." (Covetousness is the root of all evil.) First, I pronounce whence I have come, and then display my letters of authority from the Pope.[1] The seal of our

[1] The young reader will not forget that the office of the Pardoner consisted in selling indulgences from the Pope, for sins committed. This was the chief source of scandal against the Roman Catholic religion; it formed one of the grounds of Luther's tremendous attacks upon Popery, and, without doubt, mainly contributed to bring about the Reformation. As men began to increase in knowledge, they could not but feel the wickedness, as well as absurdity, of any one human being's presuming to have the power to pardon crimes committed in the face of heaven, by the sacrifice of a few worthless pence. Chaucer (who was a partisan of Wickliffe, the first eminent Christian reformer, and who flourished 160 years before Luther,) was fully alive to the gross corruption of the Romish Church, and the infamous lives of its priests; he therefore never lets slip an opportunity of satirising them, and in the present instance has, with delightful ingenuity, made his grasping Pardoner preach against '*covetousness.*' This hateful vice has been the plague-spot of all priest-craft, and too numerous instances occur which prove that the Protestant teachers of Christianity give but little heed to the divine command, that its followers shall 'take no thought as to what they shall eat, or what they shall drink, or wherewithal they shall be clothed.'

liege lord upon my patent I display, to prove my warrant; that no man, whether priest or clerk, may be so bold as to disturb me in the exercise of Christ's holy work. After this I enter upon my discourse, ever and anon mixing up with it small scraps of Latin to saffron[1] my preaching, and steer men to devotion: then I draw forth my relics, crystals, clouts, and bones; the shoulder of a holy sheep enclosed in brass, and say, "Good men and brethren, take heed to my words; if this bone be dipped in any well, and your cattle be infected with the worm, or stung, take but the water of that well and wash them, and forthwith they shall be healed: or if your sheep have the rot, let them drink one draught of the water and they shall be cured. Lay up these words of mine therefore in your hearts. If also any good man who owns cattle will, every week before cock-crow, drink a draught of that well, fasting, his store shall multiply like the flock of holy Jacob of old. Moreover, sirs, it healeth jealousy; for let a man fall into the most

---

[1] An expressive term. Saffron was used to give *colour* as well as *flavour* to confectionaries.

grievous rage, mix but his potage with that water, and he will never more suspect his wife of deceit, even though he know the truth of her fault.

'"Behold this mitten! He that will thrust his hand into this glove, (if he offer a few groats or pence to holy church,) shall find his corn multiply in seed time.

'"But of one thing I warn you, my brethren: if any one now before me in this congregation have committed a deadly sin, so that he dare not for shame be shrived of it; or if any woman, young or old, have been treacherous to her husband, such shall have no power to offer to my relics. But whoso is aware of such sin, let him come to me and offer up in the name of God, and I will absolve him from his crime by the authority of this Bull here, granted to me by his Holiness at Rome."

'By such tricks as these, my masters, have I, year by year, made a hundred marks ever since I followed the duty of a Pardoner. I stand forth in my pulpit like any learned clerk, and preach, as you have heard, to the ignorant multitude, using a hundred other tricks than I have already told. And all the while I stretch out my neck, east and west, becking upon the people, like a dove sitting on a barn. My hands and tongue I ply so briskly that it is a joy to see me at work. All my discourse is set against avarice and such cursedness, that I may make the hearers free in offering their pence—namely, to *me;* for gain is all my care, and nothing for the correction of sin: I reck not when once they are buried, although their souls be gone to the dwelling of blackness.

'For of a truth many a sermon springeth oft-time from an evil intention: some to flatter and please the hearer, and by hypocrisy to advance one's own interest; some through vain glory, and others through private hate; for when I dare not in any other manner ply my discourse, then do I sting the object of attack with my tongue, and in such a way, that if he have offended the brotherhood or myself, he shall not start at being defamed falsely; for though I do not call him forth by name, I take good care, by signs and other circumstances, that all his neighbours shall " place the saddle on the right horse." And after this fashion am I even with those who offend us; under colour of religion and an appearance of piety and truth, spitting out my venom upon them. In short, I preach of nothing but covetousness; therefore the whole burthen of my song has ever been " Radix malorum est cupiditas."

'Thus, you see, I can preach against this same vice of which I myself am guilty,—this avarice. Although, however, I be steeped to the lips in that sin, yet have I the wit to wean others from the same offence, and bring them to a sore repentance. Yet is not this my principal intent; but to root out covetousness; I preach naught else.

'Farthermore, I tell them many examples of old stories long ago; for simple and ignorant people delight in old tales—they easily retain and report them again. What! do you think that while I teach and gather gold and silver by my prayers, that I will myself live in wilful poverty? No, no,—such matter never crossed my brain; my duty is to preach from land to land, to collect all the wealth I can for mother church; I have naught to do with labour or handicraft—I am no basket-maker—no counterfeit of the Apostles: money—money and provender will I have—aye, even from the sorriest hind, or poorest widow in the village, although her children pine for it. Wine and revelry for me! and these I get in every town.

'But to conclude, my Lords and Gentlemen, it is your wish to have my story. Now, having drunk a draught of corny ale, I hope to tell you one to your liking; for, though no saint myself, I can relate a moral tale, one that I sometimes deliver from the pulpit, and so, craving your silence, I thus begin.'

In Flanders, a long while ago, there was a company of young men who committed every act of riot and debauchery—drinking, dancing, playing, and throwing of dice; night and day this was evermore their game. With abominable superfluity also they ate and drank beyond their strength, sacrificing to the Devil in his own temple, the scene of their wickedness and debauchery. The oaths they uttered were great and heinous, that it was a dreadful thing to hear them swear. The body of our blessed Lord they horribly profaned, as though they would outvie the blaspheming Jews of old; and then each would laugh at the other's sin. Sometimes, while they were in their revelry, dancing women, young and comely; fruit-girls, singers, and harp-players, sellers of wafer-cake —a wanton band—would come in and minister to their gluttony and luxury. The holy writ bear me witness that gluttony and drunkenness are the foundation of all luxury.

O gluttony!—fellest curse!—first cause of our confusion!—origin of our condemnation!— till Jesus bought our redemption again with his blood. How dearly, alas! was this misdeed purchased:—the whole world became corrupt through gluttony alone. For this vice were Adam our forefather and his helpmate driven out of Paradise to labour and sorrow. While he abstained, he dwelt in that blest abode; and when he ate of the fruit of the forbidden tree, he became an outcast to woe and pain. O gluttony! well may we beshrew thy triumph. Let a man think of the many maladies that follow upon the excess of gluttony, and he will be more measurable of his diet. Alas! the short throat, the tender mouth, cause men to labour in earth, and air, and water, from east to west, that the glutton may be served daintily with his meat and drink. Well hast thou treated this matter, Paul, our Apostle.—'Meats for the belly,' he says, 'and the belly for meats: but God shall destroy both it and them.' A foul thing is it to say,—but fouler is the deed when a man so drinks to excess that his throat becomes the common-sewer to this detested superfluity. The Apostle also says: 'Many walk, of whom I have told you often, and now tell you, even weeping, that they are the enemies of the cross of Christ; whose end is destruction, whose God is their belly.' For what is the cook's labour—with the marrow and the spicery, the herbs and leaves, the barks and roots, but to make them go softly and sweetly through the throat, and by their delights to create a newer appetite? yet, know, of a surety, that he who haunts these dainties is but dead while living in his vice.

And thou, too, O drunken man!—disfigured

is thy face, sour thy breath, and foul and odious art thou to embrace. Thou fallest down like a slaughtered swine: thy tongue is lost to thee, and all thine honest care; for drunkenness is the very sepulchre of a man's wit and discretion. He is unfit to keep counsel over whom wine has dominion. Refrain, therefore, from the alluring white and red drink, and, above all, from the strong drink of them of Spain, whose country wines have crept subtlely into our milder vintages of Rochelle and Bourdeaux; so that by the time a man has taken his three draughts, he knows not whether he be at home in Cheap, or rolling in fair Cadiz' Bay.

Having preached to you against gluttony and drunkenness, I would also forbid you the vice of gaming. Gaming is the mother of lying, deceit, treachery, and perjury: the gambler is a blasphemer of his Maker, a destroyer of man—of his own substance, and of precious time. It is a reproof and a dishonour to be held a common gambler; and the higher his condition the more abandoned is he esteemed. In every good government, and in all wise policy, the reputation of that Prince is ever held light if he be addicted to gaming. Chilon, a wise ambassador, was sent from Lacedemon to Corinth, to create an alliance with that state; and when he arrived there he found the nobles of the place all infected with the vice of gaming: so, with the least possible delay, he stole home again to his own country: for, said he, 'I will not lose my fair name, or so dishonour myself as to ally you with a nation of gamblers: send out, if you deem it meet, other ambassadors, for by my truth, I would rather die than frame for you such an alliance. Ye who have ever been glorious in honour, shall never, by any will or treaty of mine, be connected with gamesters.' Such was the speech of this true philosopher. One more example and I have done. The King of Parthia, in scorn of King Demetrius, who had been a noted gambler, sent him a pair of golden dice, signifying that he held his glory and renown in no value or reputation. Our Lords may find other diversion honest enough to drive the day away.

A word or two I would say upon oaths, both false and great. Swearing at all is an abomination, but false-swearing is infinitely more reprehensible. Our Lord has forbade all swearing, as we read in St. Matthew; but especially the holy Jeremiah has said: 'Thou shalt swear in truth, in judgment, and in righteousness:' but idle swearing is a cursed thing. The second command in the great God's table of laws is: 'Thou shalt not take the name of the Lord thy God in vain.' Such swearing is forbidden before the commission of homicide or any other crime. And, of a surety, I declare to you that vengeance will not depart from his house that is outrageous in oaths. For the love of Him, therefore, who died for us, forbear your oaths of any kind. And, now sirs, I will go on with my tale.

These three rioters I spoke of, long before the first chime of early bell, were drinking together in a tavern; and as they sat, they heard a knell going before a corpse that was being carried to the grave: when, one of them calling to the tapster lad,—' Go, and enquire,' said he, 'what corpse is that just passing by, and bring us word.'—' Sir,' said the boy, 'I need not do that, for I heard two hours before you came here. He was an old companion of yours: he was carried off suddenly last night as he sat upon his bench—drunk. There came a private thief, called DEATH, who kills all the people in this country, and with his spear striking him to the heart, he went his way without speaking a word. He has slain a thousand people this pestilence: and, master, before you come into his presence, I think it proper that you should beware of such an adversary. Be evermore ready to meet him. So my mother taught me.'

'By St. Mary,' said the tavern-keeper, 'the child says true, for this year, in a great village, about a mile hence, Death has killed both man, woman, and child. I guess his dwelling must be thereabouts. He were a wise man who should be on his guard to prevent his doing him some mischief.'

Then with a frightful oath, did this rioter say—'Is there such peril in meeting with him? —I vow to hunt him in every stile and street in the neighbourhood. Hearken, comrades— let us all three join hands, as sworn brethren, to seek out this traitor Death and slay him.'

And so, all stark mad and drunk, they staggered forth towards the village of which the taverner had spoken, swearing by the way many a grisly oath, that if they met their enemy he should not escape them.

They had scarcely reached half-a-mile from home, when, getting over a stile, they met a poor old man, who greeted them very meekly. 'What, churl,' said the proudest of the three, 'do you do here clouted up, and crawling about at your age? Why don't you die?'

This old man looked him steadily in the face, and said:—'Because I cannot find a man, although I were to walk to the Indies to seek him, who will change his youth for my great age; and, therefore, must I bear my age as long as it is the will of God I should do so. Death, alas! will not take my life: and thus I walk about like a restless wretch, and on the ground, which is my mother's door, early and late I knock with my staff, and say to her, "Dear mother, let me in. Behold how I dwindle in my body. Alas! when shall my weary bones have rest? With you, mother, would I change my coffin, that has long been my chamber companion, for a hair-cloth to wrap me in, and lie down in peace." Yet will she not grant me this boon; and, therefore, pale and withered is my face. But, sirs, it is not courteous in you to offer insult to an old man, who trespasses neither in word nor deed. The holy writ has taught you that "you shall rise before the hoary head;" and, therefore, harm not an old man now, any more than you would desire to be harmed in age, if you are allowed so long to abide. God be with you, I must go forth upon my travel.'

'Nay—nay, old churl,' said another of the gamblers, 'by St. John, we do not part so lightly. You just now spoke of that traitor "Death," that goes about this country killing all our friends. By my truth, tell us where he is, (for I take you to be his spy,) or you shall dearly abide the consequences of your refusal. I doubt not that you are leagued with him to murder us youngsters—you false thief!'

'Sirs,' said he, 'if it be your pleasure to find out "Death," turn up yon crooked path; for, upon my faith, I left him in that grove under

THE PARDONER'S TALE.

'"Sirs," said he, "if it be your pleasure to find out DEATH, turn up yon crooked path. * * * Do you see that oak? There you will meet with him."'

a tree, and there he will remain for some time; neither will he attempt to hide himself in spite of all your boasting. Do you see that oak? There you will meet with him. God preserve and mend you,' said this old man.

These three rioters ran off immediately till they came to the tree; and there they found a large heap of fine gold florins. They sought no longer after Death, so glad were they at the sight of these fair and bright coins. And down they sat by the precious hoard, when the worst of the three proposed that as fortune had sent them the treasure to live in mirth and jollity, they should spend it as lightly as it came. 'But,' said he, 'if we take all this gold home to either of our houses, we shall run the chance of being taken up for thieves, and mayhap be hanged. We had, therefore, best carry it home slyly at night; and, in the mean time, let us draw lots who shall go to the next town and buy us bread and wine, while the other two stay and watch the money.'

So, having drawn the lots, the youngest was doomed to go to the town. As soon as he was out of sight, one of the two said to the other:

'You know that we have long been sworn brothers; now, if you will listen to me, I will show how all this gold, which is to be divided among three, shall become the property of us two only.' The other said, he knew not how that could be, for their companion was aware that the money was with them two.

'Well,' said the other, 'do not betray me, and I will show you how we may bring it about. We two are stronger than one: when, therefore, he has sat down, you must get up and pretend to play with him, and while you are struggling as in game, I will yerk him under the ribs, and see that with your dagger you then do the same. Then all this gold will be shared between you and me—my dear friend! and we may do with it as we please.' So these cursed wretches agreed to murder the third.

The youngest, as he went towards the town, cast about in his mind the beauty of the florins. 'O Lord!' said he to himself, 'if I could but have all this treasure to myself, not a man under heaven would be happier than I.' Then did the great enemy of mankind put it into his head to buy poison with which he might despatch his two companions; and forth he went to an apothecary in the town, who sold him a confectionary, the smallest portion of which, to the amount of a corn of wheat, would strike a man dead before one could walk a mile.

Then this cursed villain went and purchased three bottles, into two of which he poured the poison, filling them all three with wine, and returned to his mates, thinking to carry away the gold himself by night.

What need I to proceed with my tale? As the two had contrived his death, so they murdered him; and afterward sat down to feast, proposing, when they had finished, to bury him out of the way. It so happened, however, that they took one of the bottles containing the poison, and no wretches suffered more dreadfully in their death than they. So ended the lives of these homicides, and their poisoner.—The old man they met was—'DEATH.'

THE PRIORESS'S TALE:

THE MIRACLE OF

A CHRISTIAN'S CHILD MURDERED BY THE JEWS.

'WELL SAID, my gentle master Pardoner,' quoth our host; 'and now, my Lady Prioress, by your leave, and if it be pleasant to you, I would that we should have your story. Will you vouchsafe the request, dear Lady?'— 'Gladly,' said she, and told as you shall hear.

'O Lord! our Lord! how excellent is thy name in all the world!'—for not only is thy praise sounded by men of dignity, but by the mouth of babes and sucklings are thy goodness and bounty made known. Wherefore, in praise as I best can speak of thee, and of the white lily-flower[1] which bare thee, and is ever a maiden pure and holy, I will strive to tell a tale—not that I may increase her honour, for next to her son, our Blessed Redeemer, she is the root of all bounteousness, and our soul's only help. O, maiden mother! O, bountiful mother! O, unscathed bush, that burned in the sight of Moses, who in thine humbleness broughtest down from the Deity the Holy Spirit, which alighted upon thee, of whose virtue was conceived the wisdom of the Heavenly Father, help me to tell it in thy reverence.

No tongue, O Virgin Lady! can express thy bounty, thy magnificence, thy virtue, and thy great humility: for ofttimes when we pray, thou goest before us in thy graciousness, giving to us the light of thy prayer, to guide us to thy dear and suffering Son. Weak is my skill, O blessed Queen of Heaven, to declare thy great worth, for I am but as a twelvemonth's babe; and therefore, I pray thee to

[1] The Virgin Mary was typified by the Catholics under the lily-flower, as the emblem of innocence and purity.

prompt and guide me in the tale I am now about to tell to thine honour and glory.

In the suburbs of a great city in Asia, there was established in one quarter where the Christians dwelt, a Jewry,[1] which was maintained by a Lord of that country, for the hateful purpose of villainous lucre and usury. This street was open at both ends, and at the

---

[1] That quarter of any town or city, that the Jews inhabited, was called a *Jewry*. After the destruction of their native city, and that they had become scattered over the face of the earth, prejudice ran sorely against that people; above all, in Christian countries. They became literally 'a bye-word, a taunt, and a curse.' They were sojourners in every place—not naturalised. They were rigorously punished for offences against the laws; and the laws of both God and man were constantly set aside to persecute them. They had no rest for the sole of their foot, for they could neither buy nor inherit land. Their only resource, therefore, was to get gold, seeing that they could carry that away, when the tide of injustice and cruelty ran hard against them. They were ever keen in amassing wealth, for persecution made them so; and, contrary to the commands of their own lawgiver, and of almost all civilised nations, they derived their chief source of revenue from lending money out at *usurious* interest; which means, for a larger return than five pounds for every hundred pounds lent. The law of this country, and I believe of all commercial countries, is, that no man can claim in a court of justice a larger interest than five per cent., or 105*l.* for the loan of 100*l.* By ingenuity, however, this law is broken every day by persons *not* Jews—at least in name and religion.

farther end there stood a little school, in which the children that came of Christian parents were taught the doctrines of their religion; also to read and sing.

Among these children was a widow's son, seven years old, who every day went to the school; and on his road it was his custom whenever he saw the image of the Virgin, to kneel down as he had been taught, and repeat his 'Ave Maria.'[1] And in this manner the widow instructed her little son in the worship of our Lady, the mother of Jesus; for innocent children readily receive religious precepts. And ever, when I think on this matter, do I remember thee, holy Nicholas! and thy early reverence of thy Saviour.[2]

---

[1] 'Hail, Mary! mother of Jesus!' the first words of a prayer in the Roman Catholic Liturgy.

[2] The following is the literal translation of an old legend respecting the early indications of piety manifested by this saint. 'This man's holiness, even as in future times it would be, appeared in the very cradle. For, whereas the infant on each of the other week-days sucked of the nurse's milk again and again, he, on the fourth and the sixth, (Wednesdays and Fridays), being days of abstinence, abstained, and sucked but once, and that at even-tide.' St. Nicholas is called the patron saint of children; and on that day in the calendar dedicated to his memory, it is customary with Catholics to make presents

This little child, as he sat in the school, learning his primer, heard the children who were practising their antiphones,[1] sing the 'Alma Redemptoris.'[2] And as he dared, he drew nearer and nearer, and hearkened to the tone and the words, till he was able to sing the first verse by heart. He was of so young and tender an age, that he knew not the meaning of the Latin language, in which it was written: but one day he asked an elder schoolfellow to explain the song to him in his own tongue. His schoolmate told him that he had heard say the hymn was composed in honour of the Blessed Virgin; also to entreat her to become our help and succour when we die. 'I cannot inform you any more of the matter,' said he, 'for I myself am but a small

---

to, and give entertainments to their infant acquaintance—a pretty imitation of His wisdom and sweetness of heart, who said, 'Suffer little children to come unto me, and forbid them not, for of such is the kingdom of heaven.'

[1] Antiphonal singing means, the singing of verses alternately, as in the choirs of cathedrals. The word is of Greek origin, and signifies to sing opposite to, or over-against.

[2] 'Alma Redemptoris mater!' 'Holy, kind, or cherishing mother of the Redeemer!' The beginning of one of the prayers in the Roman Catholic Liturgy.

grammarian.'—'And was this song made in reverence of the mother of Christ?' said this innocent: 'then will I be diligent to get the whole by rote before Christmas come, though I neglect my primer, and be beaten for it three times in an hour. I will learn it in worship of our Blessed Lady.' His schoolfellow taught him as they went homeward from day to day, till he knew the whole; and then he sang it well and boldly from word to word, and according with the tone.[1] Twice a day did it come from his little pipe, as he went to and from school.

As I have said, this simple child, going to and fro through the Jewry, could not forbear singing merrily by the way 'O Alma Redemptoris mater!' so strongly had the sweetness of the subject touched his heart. But our first enemy, and the enemy of all goodness—Satan, who makes his wasp's nest in Jewish hearts, arose and said, 'O Hebrews! is it a fit thing that such a boy should walk about at his pleasure, and in your despite, singing that which

---

[1] The old word for chaunt. The chaunts attributed to Pope Gregory were called the 'Gregorian tones.'

offends against our holy laws?' So from that time, the Jews conspired to put this little innocent out of the world; for which purpose, they hired a ruffian who lived in a low alley, and as the child passed by the spot, this cursed Jew seized him fast, and having cut his throat, threw his body into a pit.

But 'murder will out,' and blood proclaimed the cursed deed. The poor widow waited up all that night for her little son, and as soon as the daylight rose, she went forth, with busy thought, and face pale with fear, to seek him at his school, or where else he might perchance have staid; until, at length, she heard that he was last seen in the Jewry. With motherly yearnings, and half out of her mind, she went to every place where she might in likelihood find him, piteously praying every Jew she met to tell her if they had seen her child pass by. All told her they had not. But by the grace of her heavenly Lord, it entered into her heart that he must be cast into the pit hard by, where she was calling him by name: and O Great God! who soundest thy praises by the mouth of innocents, behold thy power!

there, where they found this little gem of martyrdom lying upright with his mangled throat, he began to sing the Alma Redemptoris so loud, that the whole place rang again.

The Christian people, who were passing through the street, came in to wonder upon this strange event; and hastily they summoned the Provost, who came without delay, and having given thanks and praise to the Father of all, he ordered those Jews into confinement.

With piteous lamentation they took up the child, and solemnly and with great honour bore him to the next Abbey, he all the way singing his little hymn. His mother swooning, lay by the body, nor could the people remove this new Rachel from his bier.

The Provost promptly condemned every Jew that was privy to the murder to a tormenting and shameful death. 'Evil shall he have,' said he, 'who evil will deserve;' therefore he ordered them to be first drawn by wild horses, and afterwards hanged.

During the celebration of mass the murdered innocent lay upon his bier before the altar; and after, when the Abbot with his convent prepared to bury him, and while the holy water was being sprinkled upon his body, he sang again, 'O Alma Redemptoris.' The Abbot, who was a holy man, began solemnly to conjure the child, and said, 'O dear child, with reverence I enjoin thee, by virtue of the Holy Trinity, to tell me the cause that thou, to all appearance murdered, ceasest not to sing.'—'My throat,' answered the little one, 'is hewn to the bone, and in the way of nature, I should long since have died; but Jesus hath ordained, for his honour and glory, and that of his heavenly mother, that I should sing the "O Alma Redemptoris mater."—With all my slender skill and might, I ever loved the blessed mother of our Lord; and when my life was about to depart from me, she came, and bade me sing this anthem, as you have heard, in my dying; and while I lifted up my voice, methought she laid a grain upon my tongue. Wherefore I sing, and needs must sing, in honour of the Blessed Virgin till that grain is taken off my tongue. And "little child," she said "when that is taken

THE PRIORESS'S TALE.

'The Abbot, who was a holy man, began solemnly to conjure the child, and said: "O dear child, with reverence I enjoin thee, by virtue of the Holy Trinity, to tell the cause that thou, to all appearance murdered, ceasest not to sing."

away, I will fetch thee away;—fear not—I will never forsake thee."'

Then this holy Abbot gently laid hold of his tongue and removed the grain, when instantly and quietly he gave up the ghost. The worthy man seeing this great miracle, wept many tears, and fell flat upon the ground, amazed and confounded. The brethren also, upon their knees, weeping, returned honour and praise to the Blessed Virgin: after which they arose and went forth, taking this infant martyr from his bier, and enclosed his little sweet body in a tomb of fair marble.

THE NUN'S PRIEST'S TALE:

THE COCK AND THE FOX.

A FABLE.

Our host next called out, with a rough familiarity, to the Nun's Priest, 'Now, Parson! draw near, Sir John,[1] and tell us something to

[1] Sir John. I know not how it has happened that in the principal modern languages, John (or its equivalent) is a name of contempt, or at least of slight. So the Italians use *Gianni*, from whence *Zani*, the Spaniards *Juan*, as *Bobo Juan*, a foolish John, the French *Jean*, with various additions; and in English, when we call a man a *John*, we do not mean it as a title of honour. Chaucer uses *Jack-fool* as the Spaniards do *Bobo Juan*, and I suppose *Jackass* has the same etymology. The title of *Sir*, or *Sire*, was usually given, by courtesy, to Priests, both secular and regular.—*Note to Tyrwhitt's Edition of the Canterbury Tales*, 1775. If the host then used the title *John* in an impertinent or contemptuous sense; that of *Sir* must also be understood as an additional piece of rudeness, because of its affectation of courtesy and respect.

gladden our hearts. Although you do ride upon a jade, man, and your beast is poor and lean; so long as he serves your turn, no matter. See that you keep a merry heart—that is the chief care of this life.'

'Yes, host,' said he, 'riding or walking, blame me if I be not merry withal.' And straightway this goodly Priest opened upon his tale.

Long ago, a poor widow, somewhat stooping with the weight of years, dwelt in a little cottage, beside a grove, standing in a dale. Ever since she had ceased to be a wife, she earned her bread in patience and simplicity: slender was her stock, and slender was her rent. With careful husbandry she supported herself and two daughters. She had three hogs, three cows, and a ewe. Smoky was her cabin, in which she ate many a frugal meal: no pungent sauce to whet her appetite, or dainty morsel entered her lips: her diet accorded with her apparel, and both were humble. She never ailed through repletion, and temperance was her only medicine. Activity and exercise were all her heart's delight; no gout prevented her from dancing, and apoplexy made not her head to tremble. Wine formed no part of her household store, but milk was her beverage; and her meals consisted of brown bread, singed bacon, and, as it might happen, an egg or two.

She had a little yard enclosed with sticks, and, on the outside, a dry ditch. In this yard she kept a cock, called Chanticleer;—a merrier crow than his was not to be heard in all the country round. He was as true to his matin hour as the abbey clock. He could tell by instinct the ascension of the equinox; and, when it had risen fifteen degrees, then would he crow so that it was a joy to hear him. His comb was ruddier than the finest coral, and embattled like a castle-tower. His bill was black, and shone like jet; his legs and toes were azure; his nails were whiter than the lily-flower; and his neck and back were burnished gold.

This gentle cock had seven hens in his train —his wives; all of various colours, of which the fairest about the throat and breast was

Dame Partlet. She was a most courteous, discreet, debonair, and companionable lady; conducting herself withal so fairly, that since the day she was a week old, she had held fast imprisoned the heart of Sir Chanticleer. What a pleasure it was to hear them singing, in sweet accord, as the bright sun began to arise:—' My love, my joy, is far in land.' [1] For, in those days, I have heard that birds and beasts could both speak and sing as we do.

It happened one day, just before the dawn, as Chanticleer sat upon his perch among his wives, and next to him fair Partlet, he began to groan in his throat like one sore troubled in a dream. And when she so heard him roar, she became alarmed, and said,—' My own dear heart! what makes you groan in this manner? truly you are a fine sleeper!—fie, for shame!' And, he answering her, said,—' Madam, I entreat you not to be uneasy; but, upon my truth, I had just now fallen into such mischief, that my heart still quakes with fear at the thought of it. Heaven send me a clean quit-

[1] The first words of a song most probably familiar to the poet's readers.

tance of my dream, and keep me safe and sound in body. Methought that I was walking up and down our yard, when I saw a beast like a hound, who would have seized upon me and put me to death. His colour was a light tawny, betwixt yellow and red, and both his ears and tail were tipped with black; his snout was sharp, and he had two sparkling eyes. The look of him still makes me ready to die. This, most likely, occasioned my groaning.'

'Away!' said she, 'fie on your faint heart! Alas! by Heaven! you have forfeited all my affection. In faith, I cannot love a coward:— for be sure, that whatever a woman may say, we all desire our husbands to be bold, wise, and free; neither a fool nor a niggard; and, above all, no braggart. How durst you for shame say to your love that anything could make you afraid?—Have you a man's beard, and not his heart? To be frightened at a dream! which, Heaven knows, is all vanity. Dreams frequently arise from fume and repletion, when the humours increase; and, no doubt, this dream which you have had to-night, came from the great overflowing of your *red choler*, which makes people dream of arrows, and of fire with ruddy flames; of red beasts that try to bite them; of contentions and strifes, and great and small red wasps:—as the humour of melancholy will cause a man to cry out in his sleep for fear of black bulls and bears, and black devils ready to snap them up. I could tell you too of other humours, that cause one much trouble in his sleep—but let them pass. Does not Cato, that wise man, say,—"Pay no regard to dreams?"'

'Now, sir,' said she, 'when you fly down from the beam, let me urge you, for the love of Heaven, to take some cooling herbs. Depend upon it I give you good advice in recommending you to clear away both choler and melancholy: and that you may lose no time, as there is not an apothecary in the town, I will inform you of a few simples that I shall find in our yard, which have the property of thoroughly purifying your blood. You are of a very choleric complexion, and must take great care when the sun comes out in its strength that you do not become full of hot humours; else, I lay a wager that you will be laid up with an ague or tertian fever. For a day or two, I would recommend your eating some worms by way of digestive before you take your alteratives[1] of laureola, centaury, or fumitory, of hellebore, spurge, or dog-wood berries, or ground-ivy, that is growing in the yard. Pick them where they grow, and eat them. Come, be merry, my dear husband! for the sake of your father's kindred do not be afraid of dreams.'

'Madam,' said he, 'gramercy of your great learning: but, nevertheless, touching that same Cato, who had such a reputation for wisdom, although he told us to "take no heed of dreams," I assure you that you may read in old books of a higher authority than ever Cato possessed, that the very reverse of his opinion is a matter of well founded experience; for that dreams are warnings both of the joys and tribulations that people are to endure in this life. The thing needs no argument; indeed the proof of it carries conviction. One of the greatest

---

[1] Alterative medicines are those, which, unperceived, restore the body from indisposition to clear health.

authors [1] we read of relates, that formerly two men went forth upon a pilgrimage; and it happened that they came into a town where there was such a congregation of people, and the lodging so scanty, that they could not find so much as a cottage in which they could remain together; they were, therefore, compelled to part company for that night, and each of them to go to his inn, and put up with such entertainment as he might find. One of them was lodged in an ox-stall; and the other, by that good luck which at times attends every one, was comfortably provided. Now it happened that during the night, he who was well-housed dreamed that the other cried out to him for help, for that he was being murdered in an ox's-stall, where he was lodged for the night. "Hasten to help me, dear brother," said he, "or I shall die." The man started from his

---

[1] Cicero [De Divinatione, b. i. c. 27.] relates this and the following story, but in a contrary order, and with so many other differences, that one might be led to suspect that he was here quoted at second hand, if it were not usual with Chaucer, in these stories of familiar life, to throw in a number of natural circumstances not to be found in his original authors.— *Note to Tyrwhitt's Edition.*

sleep, but thinking it only a dream, he took no heed of it; so, turning round, went off again. Twice, however, he dreamed the same; and the third time, his companion, as he thought, came to him, and said,—" I am now slain—behold my deep and wide gashes: arise up early on the morrow, and go to the west gate of the town, where you shall see a cart full of dung; in this my body is privately concealed. Boldly arrest that cart. My gold was the cause of my being murdered;"—and so he told him, with a pale and piteous face, every point how he was slain. And be sure that he found his dream all true: for in the morning, as soon as it was day, he went to his companion's inn, and when he came to the ox-stall he enquired after him. The ostler told him that his fellow-traveller had left the town at day-break. The survivor, bearing his dream in mind, began to suspect, and immediately went to the west gate, where he found a dung-cart exactly as the dead man had described; when he began to cry out lustily for help and vengeance, saying, that his companion lay murdered in that cart. What more need I say? The people rushed out and overturned the cart, where, in the midst of the dung, they found the dead man newly murdered.

'O good, true, and blessed God! behold, how thou dost always cause murder to betray itself! Every day do we find the saying true that "murder will out;" so loathsome and abominable to a just God is this crime, that he will not suffer it to be hidden, though it remain concealed for years. Straightway the magistrates of that time having seized the carter and ostler, and put them to the rack, they confessed their wickedness, and were both hanged.

'Thus you may see that dreams are to be feared. And in the very next chapter of the same book you may read of two who were about to take a voyage to a far country, but were detained by reason of contrary winds. One day, however, at eventide, the wind began to change; and gladly they retired to rest, thinking to set sail early on the morrow. But a strange event happened to one of the two. As he lay asleep he dreamed that a man stood by his bed-side, and ordered him to abide behind; "for if," said he, "you go to-morrow, you will be drowned." He awoke, and told his companion what had happened to him, and entreated that he would put off his voyage for that day. The other, who lay by his bed-side, began to laugh and scoff at him. "No dream," said he, "can deter my heart from attending to my concerns. I value not your dreams a straw,—they are all vanity. Men dream of things that never did or will come to pass. But since I see you are inclined to lose your tide, fare you well." And so he took his leave and went away. But, before he had gone half his course, I know not by what chance it came about, the ship split, and both vessel and man went to the bottom in the sight of others sailing in company. Therefore, dear Partlet, by these old examples you may see that no one should be reckless of dreams, for many a one is to be sorely dreaded.

'But let us drop all this, and think only of mirth and jollity. Madam Partlet, so happy am I when I look upon the beauty of your face—you have so fine a scarlet round your eyes, that it banishes all my fear; for truly may we say, "In principio mulier est hominis confusio," (Madam, the meaning of this Latin is, "Woman is man's joy and delight,"[1]) for when I feel by night your soft side, as we are seated upon our narrow perch, I am so full of comfort and happiness, that I defy all dreams and augury. And with that word he and all his hens flew down from the beam, for it was day: then with a chuck he began to call them round him, for he had found some corn in the yard. Right royal he was, and had lost all his fear. He looked about him as grimly as a lion, and roamed up and down upon his toes, disdaining to set his feet upon the ground. And when he had discovered a grain of corn, he chucked, and all his wives ran to him.

And so I leave our Chanticleer at his pasture, like a royal prince in his banqueting hall, and turn to relate his adventures. In the opening of the month of May it happened, that, as Chanticleer, in all the pride of his seven wives, who were walking by his side, cast up his eyes to the bright sun, who had made somewhat

---

[1] The impudent wag! he knew that Dame Partlet was no scholar, or she would have told him that the translation o the saying was, 'In the beginning woman was man's *confusion.*'

more than twenty degrees in the sign of Taurus, he knew by instinct that it was six o'clock; and then he sounded the hour with his merry note. 'Madam Partlet,' said he, 'my world's bliss, only hearken how those happy birds are singing, and see the fresh flowers how they grow!—all these things fill my heart with such joy and comfort!' But, suddenly a sorrowful mishap befel him, (for grief ever follows upon the heels of joy,) and heaven knows that worldly joy has soon fled—a chronicler may safely note this down for a sovereign truth. Now, hearken to me, gentles all, and wise.—The story I am now telling is as true as that book of Sir Launcelot du Lake, which all the women hold in so great reverence.

A Fox, full of sly iniquity, who for three years had dwelt in the grove hard by, that same night broke through the hedge into the yard where fair Chanticleer, with his wives, was accustomed to repair, and in a bed of cabbages he lay quietly till about nine o'clock, watching his opportunity to fall upon him. O, Chanticleer! evil befall the morning on which you flew from your perch into that yard. Full well had you been warned in your dream that this day was unpropitious to you—but what has been ordained, needs must come to pass. You took counsel of your wife, and the advice of women is apt to be luke-warm or cold. Woman's advice first ' brought us all our woe, with loss of Paradise ' to Adam, where he led a merry life and at his ease. As I may offend many, however, by my disparagement of women's discretion in giving advice, I pass the matter over—these are the Cock's words, not my own : I can divine no harm in woman.

Dame Partlet and all her sisters were bathing themselves in the dust against the sun, and Chanticleer singing as merrily as a mermaid, when happening to cast his eye upon a butterfly among the cabbages, he was aware of this Fox crouching upon his belly. He had no idea then of crowing ; but up he started and cried out—' Cok ! cok ! cok !' like one heart-stricken with fright : for it is natural in a beast to flee from his enemy, although he had never before set eyes on him. So Chanticleer would have made off, but that the Fox said quickly, ' Gentle Sir, what are you going to do ? Are you afraid of me, who am your friend? Worse than a fiend were I, if I should offer you any harm or villainy. I come not to pry into your counsel, but only for the purpose of hearing you sing; for by my faith you have as merry a note as any angel in heaven; and withal you have a finer feeling for music than Boethius himself, or any songster. My lord, your father, (heaven rest his soul!) and your mother too, in her gentility, have both been at my house, to my great delight, and most happy, Sir, should I be to please you. But speaking of singing, I will say, that, excepting yourself, I never heard any one like your father in a morning: he put his heart into every thing he sang; and to give his voice the more strength he would strive so, that it made him wink his eyes with the loudness of his note, standing too upon tiptoe and stretching forth his long small neck. And then he had such judgment that no man any where could surpass him either in song or wisdom. I have read in the verses of Dan[1] Burnel the ass, of a cock, that,

---

[1] Dan was formerly a title of distinction commonly given to monks.

THE NUN'S PRIEST'S TALE.

Our chanticleer stood high upon his toes, stretching his neck, and, holding close his eyes, began to crow with all his might. Up starts Dan Russell, and catches him by the gorge.'

because a priest's son gave him a knock upon his leg, he contrived to make him lose his benefice: but certainly there is no comparison betwixt the wisdom and discretion of your father and his subtlety. Now then, Sir, for charity's sake be pleased to sing, and let us see if you can counterfeit your father.'

This Chanticleer, like a man unconscious of treachery, began to beat his wings, so ravished was he with all this flattery. Alas! for you Lords! many a false flatterer have you in your courts, who please you more than he that will tell you nothing but the truth. Beware, Lords, of the treachery of such dependants.

Our Chanticleer, standing high upon his toes, stretching his neck, and holding close his eyes, began to crow with all his might. Up starts Dan Russell[1] and catches him by the gorge, bearing him off on his back toward the wood, for as yet there was no one to follow him.

O Fate, that may not be avoided! alas that Chanticleer flew from his perch!—alas, that his wife had no faith in dreams! On a Friday, too, fell all this mischance.

---

[1] Chaucer possibly calls the fox *Russell*, from his red, or *russet* colour.

O Geoffry,[1] dear, sovereign master of the poetic art, who, when thy worthy King Richard was slain, so sorely bewailed his death, why have I not thy learning to chide as thou didst this same unlucky day? (for on a Friday also was he killed.) Then would I show you how to lament the painful fate of Chanticleer.

When Troy was sacked, and Pyrrhus with his stern sword, having seized old Priam by his grey beard, slew him, the ladies of the palace made not so great cry and lamentation as did all the hens in the close when they witnessed the spectacle of their beloved Chanticleer.— Above them all shrieked Dame Partlet, louder than the wife of Asdrubal at the death of her husband, when the Romans burned Carthage. So full of fury and torment was that noble-minded woman, that with a stedfast heart she wilfully rushed into the fire, giving herself for a burnt-offering to her Lord. But to my tale again.

The simple widow and her two daughters heard the woful shouting of the hens, and out

---

[1] Geoffry de Vinsauf, author of a poem on the death of Richard the First.

they started, when they saw the Fox making towards the wood bearing the cock upon his back. 'The fox! the fox!' they cried, and after him they scoured; many neighbours also came out with sticks. Out ran Col the dog, and Talbot and Garland; and Malkin with her distaff in her hand: away ran the cow and calf; the very hogs too scoured off, and ran ready to break their hearts at the barking of the dogs and the shouting of the people. They all yelled like fiends in torment. The ducks screamed—the geese flew over the trees, and even a swarm of bees scrambled out of their hive. So hideous was the noise, that Jack Straw[1] and his men, when they were going to kill a Fleming, were not so outrageous as these in pursuing the Fox. Horns and trumpets they brought out, and shrieked and hooped as if heaven and earth were coming together.

And now I pray you to mark how suddenly Madam Fortune will, upon occasion, check the hope and pride of her enemies! This cock as he lay upon the Fox's back, in a deadly fright

---

[1] See the History of the Reign of Henry VI.

said to him,—'If I were you, Sir, I would turn again upon these churls, and bid them sheer off, with a pestilence; for, having reached the wood-side, you would make a meal of your cock in spite of their heads.'

'And so I will, i'faith,' answered the Fox; and as he opened his mouth in speaking, suddenly the cock broke away from him and flew up into a tree.

When he saw his prey was gone, 'Alas! Chanticleer,' said he, 'I did you an ill turn in frightening you so when I brought you out of the yard; but, Sir, I did not do it with a wicked intention; come down, and I will explain every thing.'

'No—no!' said the cock, 'beshrew us both —and hang me up body and bones, if ever you cheat me a second time: your flattery shall no more get me to sing and wink my eyes; for, ill betide him who winks when he should be looking about him.'

'Nay then,' said the Fox, 'heaven send him bad luck who will keep jangling when he should be silent'—and off he brushed.

And here, gentlemen, you see the evil of

thoughtlessness and trusting to flattery. You, who look upon the fable of a fox, a cock, and a hen as so much folly, will do well to give heed to the moral of it,—take the grain and leave the chaff.

THE CANON-YEOMAN'S TALE.

THE STORY OF THE ALCHYMIST.

PROLOGUE.

BEFORE we had ridden five miles after the conclusion of the last tale, a man overtook us at Boughton-under-Blee, wearing a black cloak, and under it a white surplice. His hack, which was a dapple grey, was all in a lather;—it seemed as though it had galloped hard for three miles at the least. His Yeoman's beast, too, was in the same condition; the foam stood so high upon its breast-plate, that it was spotted like a magpie. The rider seemed accoutred for a journey, for on the crupper behind him he carried a double portmanteau. The master rode light for summer travelling. I began to consider of what description was his quality, till I perceived that his cloak was sewed to the hood, when I guessed him to be some Canon. His hat hung down his back by a lace, because he had ridden at such a rate. He had put a dock-leaf under his hood to keep it from the moisture of his head, and that from the heat of the cloth. His forehead dropped like the retort of a still. When he had come up with us he called out, 'God save this jolly company! I have ridden at a sharp rate to overtake you in order that I might join your society.'

His Yeoman was also equally courteous, and said, 'Gentlemen, I saw you ride out of your inn early this morning, and gave my master notice of the circumstance, for he loves amusement.'—'Friend,' said our host, 'good luck betide you for the warning you gave your master: he looks to be a wise man, and, I doubt not, is a jocund one. Tell me—can he tell us a merry tale or two to please our company?'—'Who, Sir? my master? Aye truly, Sir, he has anything but enough of mirth and jollity; and, Sir, if you knew him as well as I do, you would wonder to see in how many ways and how craftily he can work. Many a great undertaking has he taken in hand, which it were full hard for any one here to bring about, unless by his assistance. Simply and homely as he there rides amongst you, his acquaintance would turn to the profit of any one. I dare lay all I am worth that not one of you would forego his acquaintance for the good he could bring you. He is a passing man, and of high discretion; and so I give you warning.'

'Well—but,' said our host, 'is he a clerk, or what? Tell us what he is.'

'Nay he is greater than a clerk,' said the Yeoman; 'and in few words I will show you some of his skill. My Lord, here, I say, is master of such an art; (I can't let you into the whole secret of his craft, although I help him in his work,) that all the ground we have ridden over till we come to Canterbury he could pave with silver and gold.'

'Bless us!' said our host, 'but this is a marvellous thing to me, that, with such a gift your master should set so little store by his worship. Why, his dress is so shabby and torn that it is not worth a farthing. If your master's power is equal to your description, why does he go about in so slovenly a fashion?'

'Why?' said the Yeoman, 'why do you ask me? The reason is, I believe that he is too wise. As our clerks say, "That which is overdone turns to a fault." So in this matter I think him foolish; for your men of overmuch sense are apt to misuse it; and that —heaven mend him!—is the case with my master.'

'Well—no matter for his dress,' said our host, 'but, good Yeoman, since you know somewhat of your Lord's skill, pray tell us what and how he works: and where do you live?'

'In the suburbs of a town,' said he, 'among corners and blind lanes; where thieves and those of their kind hold their fearful residence; men who dare not show their faces by day. In such places, if I must say the truth, we live.'

'Well, but again,' said our host, 'what makes your face so discoloured?'

'Why, my complexion is changed with blowing hot fires. I don't pass my time in looking at myself in the glass, but in hard labour. We are always poring over the furnace; and yet withal I do not find that we gain our desires. We persuade people to lend us money and gold, you see, and make them believe that we can turn one pound into two. And yet, with all our trying and groping, there's no such thing. That science is so far beyond us, that, swear how we may that we shall overtake it, it slips away, and will make beggars of us at last.'

While the Yeoman was thus talking away, the Canon drew near, and heard what he was saying, for he was always suspicious when people were in conversation: as Cato says, 'He that is guilty believes that every speech refers to himself.' Therefore he said to his Yeoman, 'Hold your peace, or you shall dearly abide your folly. You are slandering me in this company, and discovering what you ought to conceal.'

'Tell on—tell on,' said our host, 'whatever betide; don't reckon his threats at a farthing.'

'I'faith,' said he, 'I do but little.' And when this Canon found that his Yeoman would betray his secret, he fled away for very sorrow and shame.

'Aha!' said the Yeoman, 'now we'll have some fun. Since he is off I'll tell you all I know about him. The foul fiend catch him; for never more, I promise you, will I join with him for a penny or pound. Shame and trouble follow him that first brought me to that game. I feel it, say what they will of me: and yet for all my sorrow, and hard labour, and misdeeds, I could not bring myself to leave the trade. I wish I could tell you all that belongs to that art; some of it, however, I can tell!; and since my master is gone, I will not spare but relate all I know.'[1]

---

[1] It is worthy of remark, that in this early stage of science, Chaucer should have had the good sense to see through the folly of the art of Alchymy, or the power of turning baser metals into gold; which for ages deluded so many people, shrewd ones as well as simple. So lately even as in the time of Steele the wild pursuit was not wholly abandoned; for the author of the Tatler and Spectator, who was acute enough in perceiving the weaknesses of his fellow mortals, could himself be induced to lose that time in the attempt, which a steady employment of his pen, and prudent economy of its proceeds,

THE CANON-YEOMAN'S TALE.

Although I lived with this Canon for seven years, yet am I no nearer to the secret of the art he practised. All that I possessed in the world have I lost by it; and so indeed have many more than I. At that time I was accustomed to be gay of heart, and fresh in my clothing: now may I go with a hose for the covering of my head. And whereas my colour was fresh and rosy, now its hue is wan and leaden. Hard labour, too, has bleared my eyes. Such is the advantage of increase and multiplication! That slippery science has left me so bare, that wherever I go I reap no benefit. So deeply, too, am I in debt, from the gold I have borrowed, that while I live I shall never be a free man. Let every one take warning by my error; for, whoever enters upon the same pur-

---

would have superseded. Steele had the power of working a greater miracle than that of turning lead into gold. He needed but to write words upon paper. The leaden thoughts of some writers, and their success in making account of them, would lead one to conclude that the science of alchymy is no other than an allegory.

suit and follows it up, he may count his gain for loss: empty will be his purse, and empty his wits. And when, through his madness and folly, he has hazarded and lost his own wealth, then he excites others to the same headlong course; for joy is it to bad natures to have fellowship in pain and disease. This saying was taught me by a clerk: but let that pass; and now to speak of our handicraft.

When we enter upon our fantastic avocation, we put on a face of prodigious wisdom, using none but quaint and learned terms, and all the while my business is to blow the fire till my heart faints within me. I need not detail the proportions of every material that we work upon; such as five or six ounces of silver, as may be, or trouble myself and you with the names, such as orpiment,[1] burnt bones, iron scales and fragments, ground all together to a fine powder; and how all is placed in an earthen pot; putting in before hand salt and pepper, the whole being well closed with a glass receiver that none of the air may escape: and of

---

[1] A fossil of a bright and beautiful yellow colour, like pure gold.

the gentle fire that is made; and of the care and toil that we take in sublimating our materials, and in amalgamating and calcining quicksilver, that is called crude mercury. For all this, our sleights of hand come to no good conclusion: our orpiment and sublimated mercury; our white lead ground on marble, certain ounces of each, are of no avail; our labour is all in vain. Neither our spirits' ascension nor our materials may in our work avail us any thing; for lost is all our labour, and all the cost expended upon it is gone too.

Many other matters also appertain to our craft, though, being an unlettered man, I cannot rehearse them in their proper order; yet I will tell them as they arise in my mind,—as bole ammoniac, verdigris, borax, and earthen and glass vessels; descensories,[1] vials, crucibles, and sublimatories;[2] cucurbites[3] and alembics, and other such stuff, dear enough at the price of a leek. Rubifying waters, ox-gall and

[1] Vessels used in chemistry for the extracting of oils.

[2] Vessels used in sublimation; that is, separating certain parts of a body, and driving them to the top of a vessel in the form of a very fine powder.

[3] A vessel shaped like a gourd, (so called from the Latin for that fruit) used in distillation.

arsenic, sal-ammoniac, and brimstone; with herbs a long list, as agrimony, valerian, and moonwort, and a hundred others. Our lamps burning night and day, and our calcining furnaces to bring about our craft—if possible: our waters of albification, with unslaked lime, chalk, white of egg, various powders, ashes, manure and clay, saltpetre and vitriol, salt of tàrtar, alkali, and prepared salt; clay made with horse and man's hair; oil of tartar, alum, glass, yeast, wort, and argoil;[1] red arsenic, and other imbibing and incorporating materials; our silver citrination, our cementing and fermenting; our ingots and vessels for assaying the metals, and many other things besides.

I will tell you also, as I have heard my master name them, of the four spirits and seven bodies. The first spirit is called quicksilver, the second orpiment, the third sal-ammoniac, and the fourth brimstone. Of the seven bodies, Sol is gold, Luna silver, Mars iron, Mercury is quicksilver, Saturn lead, Jupiter is tin, and Venus copper. But I forgot to speak of our corrosive waters, and metal filings, of mollify-

[1] Potter's clay.

ing bodies, and of their induration; oils, ablutions, and fusible metal; all which to enumerate would exceed the largest book that ever was written. So let them be, for I must come shortly to my story.

Before the pot is placed upon the fire, my master (and no one but himself) tempers the metals; and though he has such a name for skill (now he is gone I will say it boldly), he sometimes makes sore blunders; for it often happens that the vessel will burst, and then good-bye to all our labour. These metals are so violent in their operation, that stone walls cannot resist them. Some are blown into the ground, or scattered about the floor, or fly through the roof, and in this way have we lost many a pound. Then comes the disappointment and chiding of the adventurers, some complaining that the metal was too long upon the fire; others of the blowing: (then would I begin to quake, for that was my office.) Pshaw! cries a third, you know nothing about it:—it was not properly tempered. The cause of it all, says a fourth, is, that the fire was not made with beechwood. All I know of the matter, myself, was, that there was a terrible outcry and strife among us. Then would my master say, 'Come, come, there is no more to do, but to pluck up our hearts and sweep the floor. I am sure the pot was cracked; but I can soon remedy all this mischief.'

The rubbish being all swept into a heap and put into a canvas and sifted, one of them would say, 'Here is some of our metal, though not all of it; and though this misfortune has befallen us, another chance may prove a lucky one. We *must* put out our money to a venture; the merchant is not always prosperous; one time his wealth is swallowed by the sea, and another it comes safely to land.'

'Peace, peace!' would my master then say; 'the next time I will contrive better—only trust to my wits—there *was* some mistake somewhere.' Then again, one would say the fire was too hot; but, too hot or too cold, this I know, that we were all at fault, and never got what we were seeking: and so in our madness every one seemed to himself a Solomon:— but all is not gold that shines like gold; nor is every apple, fair to the eye, good at heart:

and so it was amongst us; he that seemed the wisest, proved the greatest fool; and he a thief, who appeared most true; all which you will find by the time I have concluded my tale.

There was a Canon dwelt among us, who would have infected a whole city, be it as large as Nineveh, or any three such. His tricks and infinite falseness no one could describe, though he were to live a thousand years: he was peerless, in this world, of falsehood and treachery. So artfully would he wind his words, that he would beguile any one of his senses, although he were a fiend like himself; and therefore men have ridden miles to make his acquaintance, not knowing the treachery of his nature. In London, too, lived a Priest, an annualler,[1] and had resided there many years. So pleasant and serviceable was he to the good woman where he lodged, that she would suffer him to pay nothing for his board and clothes, however gaily he might appear. He had plenty of money to spend, and this brought our false Canon to him one day, who entreated that he

---

[1] A Priest employed solely to sing annuals, or anniversary masses for the dead, without having any cure of souls.

would lend him a certain sum, a mark or so, promising to pay it again. 'In three days,' said he, 'I will restore it, and if you find me false, hang me up by the neck.'

The Priest gave him the mark, and the Canon, thanking him over and over again, took his leave. On the third day he brought back the money, and gladdened the heart of the Priest. 'It is no inconvenience to me,' said he, 'to lend whatever I have to one who is so punctual to his promise in returning it; I could never say nay to such a man.'

'What!' answered the Canon, 'shall I break my word! No, no, Sir, truth is a thing I shall ever hold sacred to the day that I creep into my grave: God forbid it should be otherwise. Believe this as surely as your creed; and I thank God to be enabled to say it: never was the man ill paid that at any time lent me his silver or gold, and never falsehood found shelter in my heart. And now, Sir, since you have been so kind to me; to quit you of your gentleness, I will show you, if you are inclined to learn, how I work in philosophy.'

'You, Sir!' said the Priest 'will you?

Most heartily do I accept your offer, and thank you.'

'Doubtless, at your command, Sir,' answered the Canon. How true is the old saying, that 'Proferred service hath an ill intent;' and that I shall soon verify in this Canon.

Perhaps you may be thinking, Sir Host, that this man was my own master, but indeed it was another Canon; my lord had not a hundredth part of his subtlety: many are the folks, it is true, that he has betrayed; and whenever I speak of his falsehood, my cheeks burn with shame: redness I know I have little enough, for the fumes of the metals have discharged the colour from my face.

'Sir,' said this Canon, 'let your man go and purchase two or three ounces of quicksilver; and when he returns, you shall behold a more wonderful sight than ever met your eyes.' The servant went, and soon brought the quicksilver; when the Canon took the three ounces, and bid the man bring coals that he might begin his work. The fire being properly laid, the Canon took a crucible from his bosom, and showed it to the Priest. 'Take this instrument,' said he, 'and put into it an ounce of the quicksilver, and begin the labour of a philosopher. There are very few men to whom I would show so much of my science; but you shall see that I will destroy this metal, and turn it into as fine silver as that which is in your purse. Here is a costly powder that will make all good, for it is the cause of all the craft that I shall show you. Send your man out of the room, and shut the door, that no one may see us at our philosophy.' The master having dismissed his servant, and shut the door, they both went busily about their work.

The Priest, at the Canon's bidding, set the crucible on the fire, and began to blow it, and the Canon threw into the crucible a powder, made up of I know not what,—chalk or glass —not worth a fly, to blind the priest, at the same time bidding him heap the coals above the crucible; 'for, as a proof of my love for you,' said the Canon, 'your own hands shall achieve the whole work that is to be done.'

Glad was the simple Priest, and attended to all he was bidden. So, while he was busy, his treacherous companion took out from his bosom a beech coal, which he had privately hollowed out, and put into it some silver filings, stopping them in with wax. This he kept concealed in his hand, and while the Priest was busily heaping the coals; 'My good friend,' said he, 'the fire is not piled as it should be, let me manage it, while you wipe the moisture from your face.' And as the Priest was using the cloth, the Canon slipped the coal into the crucible, and began to blow the fire. 'Now let us sit down,' said he, 'and have something to drink, and I answer for it, that all will soon be right.' When the beech coal was burnt, the filings naturally fell down into the crucible, the Priest all the while perfectly innocent of the trick passed upon him.

When the Alchymist saw his time, he desired the Priest to rise up, and stand by him: 'And, as I suppose,' said he, 'you have no ingot by you, go and bring me a piece of chalk, and I will make it into the same form as an ingot. Bring also a bowl or pan full of water, and you shall see how our undertaking

THE CANON-YEOMAN'S TALE.

'" My good friend," said he, "the fire is not piled as it should be: let me manage it, while you wipe the moisture from your face."'

will thrive. Yet, in order that you may entertain no suspicion of me, during your absence, I will not leave your side, but go and return with you.' So they fastened the chamber door, taking with them the key.

When they returned, our Canon took the chalk, and fashioned it into the shape of a thin plate of silver that lay concealed in his sleeve, which he cunningly contrived, undetected by the Priest. This he slipped into the crucible on the fire, and after due time turned the whole into the water, desiring his dupe to put in his hand and search, for that he hoped he might find some silver:—and what else should there be? A plate of silver is a silver plate, all the world over!

The Priest did as he was told, and certainly brought out the metal which the Canon had put there. Who was so happy, now, as this poor deluded man? 'Heaven's choice blessings reward you, Sir Canon,' said he, 'and misfortune cleave to me but I will be yours in every thing, if you do but vouchsafe to teach me this noble craft.'

'I will make a second trial,' said the Canon,

'that you may take notice, and become expert in the art, and at your need, essay to do the same at any future time during my absence. Take an ounce of quicksilver, and proceed exactly as you have done with this, which has now become pure silver metal.'

The Priest blithely set about his work as the Canon directed him, who in the meanwhile had ready in his hand a hollow stick, at the end of which was enclosed just an ounce, and no more, of silver filings. These, as before with the coal, were stopped in with wax. And while the Priest was busied about his work, the Canon, with stick in hand, began to cast the powders into the fire. Then stirring up the materials in the crucible, the wax naturally melted, and the contents quickly dropped out.

When the Priest, suspecting nothing but truth, was a second time beguiled, he was so rejoiced, that I cannot describe his mirth and gladness; and, forthwith, he proffered his all to the Canon—body and goods. 'Aye, aye!' said the cheat, 'poor though I am, you will find me very skilful. There is still more behind. Have you any copper in the house?'

—Yes, Sir,' said he, 'I believe there is.'—' Else go and buy some quickly.' He went his way, and returned with the copper, of which the Canon weighed out an ounce. This he placed in the crucible, and set on the fire, casting in the powder, and made the Priest blow the coals, and cower down over his work as before. Afterwards he turned it all into the water, and put in his own hand. In his sleeve, as you have heard me tell already, he had another plate of silver; this he slily took out, and left at the bottom of the pan; and as he groped and rumbled about in the water, he privately took out the ounce of copper, concealing it away. 'Now,' said he, 'stoop down, and help me as I did you the last time, put your hand in, and see what is there.' The Priest, of course, took out the piece of silver. Then the Canon said, 'Let us now go with these three plates to some goldsmith, and know if they be worth any thing; for, by my hood, I hold that they will prove to be fine silver.' The pieces were put to trial by the goldsmith, and pronounced to be what they ought to be.

No one was now more glad than this besotted

Priest. The roosting bird was not happier at the approach of day; the nightingale at May-tide was never better inclined to sing; or lady more mirthful in her caroling, or to speak of love and womanhood; or knight in arms to achieve a hardy deed, that he might stand in his lady's grace, than was our Priest to be taught this craft. 'Tell me I beseech you,' said he, 'for the love of heaven, what will be the cost of this receipt?'

'By our Lady,' said the Canon, 'it's dear. I assure you that no man in England but myself and a Friar can do what you have seen.'

'No matter, Sir,' said the Priest, 'but tell me, for heaven's sake, what I shall pay you.'

'Well then, I tell you again the secret is a dear one; but Sir, since you desire to possess it, in one word, you shall pay me forty pounds; and I should have charged you more, but for your former friendship towards me.'

The Priest quickly brought out the forty pounds in nobles,[1] and gave them to the Canon for his receipt.

---

[1] A noble was worth 6s. 8d.

'Now, Sir Priest,' said he, 'I am only desirous to have my craft kept close; as you love me, therefore, let it remain a secret; for if it were made public, people would so envy me and my philosophy, that they would certainly take my life.'

'Heaven forbid what you say,' replied the Priest; 'I had rather spend all the wealth I have (I were mad else), than you should fall into such mischief.'

'For your good will, Sir,' answered the Canon, 'may you have a prosperous trial of your skill; and so farewell, and many thanks.' —He went his way, and from that day forth the Priest never saw him more. And when he proved the value of his receipt—farewell!—it was naught. So was he befooled and cheated. Thus ends my tale; and God grant to every one an end of his troubles.

THE COOK'S TALE

OF

GAMELIN.

LISTEN to me, Lords, and you shall hear tell of a doughty Knight whose name was Sir John of Bounds. He owned large store of game, with three sons. The eldest was of an evil disposition, and early began to give proof of it. His brothers loved their father, and stood in awe of him; but the eldest deserved his curse, and, at the last, he received it. Although this good old Knight had lived to a great age, death overtook, and sorely handled him. While he lay in his last sickness he was much perplexed to think how his children should fare when he was gone.

All the land he possessed was his own by

purchase; and earnestly he wished that it should be equally divided among the three. He therefore sent, by word of letter, to skilful Knights in the country, desiring them to help him parcel out his lands, and apportion them fairly; adding, moreover, that if they would see him alive, they must set forth quickly.

As soon as the Knights heard of his sickness, they rested neither night nor day till they came, where he lay quietly abiding the will of God.

'My Lords,' said the good old Knight, 'I may no longer remain here, for, by the will of God, death is drawing me down to the ground.'

They all pitied him in his helpless plight, telling him not to be cast down, for that he might still see the end of his suffering.

'An end of my suffering God may send,' said he, 'but I shall not see it; for the love you bear me, therefore, Lords, divide my lands among my three sons; and deal them not amiss, my friends: and forget not Gamelin, my youngest: regard him equally with his elders; for it is seldom that you see an heir who will help his brother as he ought.'

The Knights left the sick man, and went in to counsel upon the division of his land, which they portioned out to the two eldest, and to Gamelin they awarded nothing, saying, that his brothers could give him his due when he came of age. Having so dealt out the property, they returned and told the Knight how they had decided, who liked not their judgment, but said angrily, 'By Saint Martin! I swear, for all that you have done, the land is still mine, and I shall deal it according to my own will. John, my eldest son, shall have my father's inheritance, amounting to five ploughs of land: my second shall also have five ploughs, which I myself acquired by the labour of my own right hand; and all my other purchases of ground, with my good steeds, I bequeath to Gamelin: and I beseech you, who know the law regarding landed property, that, for the love of Gamelin, this my bequest may stand.' Soon after this he lay as still as a stone, and when his hour came, he died.

No sooner was the old Knight laid beneath the grass, than the eldest brother beguiled the young one, and took into his hands the management of all his inheritance, and Gamelin himself, to clothe and feed. Barbarous and savage was his fare; his lands and houses, parks and woods, were let away, and nothing that belonged to him went on well.

So long did young Gamelin dwell in his brother's hall that he had reached the age of manhood; when the strongest in the place began to fear his prowess. Neither young nor old, however courageous, cared to anger him. One day as he was standing in his brother's premises, thoughtfully handling his beard, he remembered how all his lands lay waste and desolate, and his fair large oaks were hewn down; his parks broken in, and deer all rived; and how, of all his good steeds, not one was left to him: his houses too, were going to ruin; and young Gamelin thought to himself, 'All this cannot be right.'

At this moment his brother came walking in with a proud and stately air, and said to him, 'Is the dinner ready?' Then poor Gamelin's wrath arose, and he swore a bitter oath; 'You shall go and bake your meats yourself,' said he, 'for I will not be your cook.'—'What!

brother Gamelin,' said the other, 'do you answer me so? why, you never spoke such a word as this before!'

'By my faith,' said Gamelin, 'I find the need to do so; I have never yet heeded all the injuries I have received: my parks are broken up, and my deer taken away; none of my good horses with their furniture is left; all that my father bequeathed to me is gone to rack and ruin; a curse, therefore, light upon you, brother John!'

'Stand still, and hold your peace, you gadling,'[1] answered John, 'you shall be glad enough to have your food and clothing;—what have you to do with lands?'

'Evil befall him,' said Gamelin, 'who calls me gadling. Brother John, I am no worse gadling than yourself, and am no worse man; I was born of a lady, and my father was a Knight.'

John dared not stir one foot nearer to him, but he called his men, and desired them to 'go

---

[1] Gadling—an idle vagabond. The brother calls him this name on account of its similarity to that of *Gamelin*, as well as through contempt.

and beat that boy, and teach him to answer better another time.'

'If I must needs be beaten,' said Gamelin, 'you shall be the one to do it.' Yet his brother in furious passion ordered his men to bring their staves. Gamelin was aware of their coming, and, looking about him, saw a stake under a wall; and, being nimble, he leaped towards them, and drove all his brother's men in a heap. He looked like a wild lion, and laid on in good earnest; which, when his brother saw, he ran away, and locked himself in a garret;—so Gamelin with his staff made them all aghast. Then he sought his brother where he had fled, and saw him looking out of the window. 'Come down, brother,' said he, 'and I will teach you to play at buckler.' But while he held that staff he would not come near him. 'Throw away your weapon,' said he, 'and I will make peace with you and never anger you more.'—'I must needs be wroth,' said Gamelin, 'seeing that you would make your men break my bones. If it had not been for the strength of my own arm to drive them before me, they would have done me a mischief.'

'I meant you no harm,' said John, 'but only to try your strength who are so young: do not, therefore, be angry, for I were loth to see you hurt.'

'Come down, then,' said Gamelin, 'and grant me my boon; but one thing will I demand, and we shall be quickly agreed.' So down came the fickle and treacherous brother, but he stood in awe of Gamelin's trusty staff. 'Ask me now your boon,' said John, 'and blame me if it be not quickly granted.'

'Brother of mine,' answered Gamelin, 'if we are to be one, you must restore all that my father bequeathed to me: you must do this if we are to have no more strife.'

'That you shall have, Gamelin, I pledge you my oath, all and more than your father's bequest if you desire it. Your land, that now lies fallow, shall be well cropped, and your houses raised again.' So spoke the Knight, but only with his mouth; he thought only of falsehood, as was his nature; but Gamelin had no guile. His brother kissed him, and they were friends.

Alas for young Gamelin! he little knew of

the treason that his brother was plotting against him with that kiss.

There happened to be in that quarter a wrestling match for a prize ram and a ring: and Gamelin had a mind to go to it and prove his strength. 'Brother,' said he, 'you must lend me a horse to-night, fresh at the spurs; I must go on an errand here beside.'

'Choose the best horse in my stall, brother; but tell me where you are going.' Gamelin told him his intent, adding, 'how much worship will it be to us if I could bring home to the hall the prize ram and ring.'

A fleet horse was saddled, and Gamelin, having buckled on his spurs, bestrode him and hied away to the wrestling. When he had gone, his false brother locked the gate, and prayed heaven that he might break his neck at the match.

As soon as he arrived at the wrestling place, he alighted and stood upon the grass. And there he heard a Franklin lamenting and bitterly wringing his hands. Gamelin asked the cause of his grief, and if any one could help him out of his care.

'Alas!' said the Franklin, 'that ever I was born; for I have lost two brave sons. The champion here has slain them. I would give ten pounds, and more, could I meet with a man to handle him in kind.

'My good man,' said Gamelin, 'will you have this well done? Hold my horse while my man draws off my shoes; and do you help him to keep my clothes and my horse, and I will go into the place and look how I may speed.'

'So be it,' replied the Franklin, 'and I will be your man to draw off your shoes: and take no thought of your clothes or your horse:—go forth, and heaven speed you.'

Barefoot and ungirt, Gamelin came into the ring, and all wondered, that knew him, how he dared adventure against so doughty a champion; who, starting up, advanced quickly towards him and said, 'Who is your father, youngster? forsooth, you are a great fool to come here.'

'You knew my father full well; his name was Sir John of Bounds, and I am Gamelin.'

'Right well I knew your father,' answered the champion, 'and yourself, while you were a young boy, for a turbulent fellow.'

'Now, then, that I am older, you shall find me more.'

'Welcome,' said the champion; 'come once within my gripe, and you shall not escape.'

It was night, and the bright moon was shining, when the two wrestlers came together. The champion cast about to throw his fellow, but he stood still, and bade him do his best. 'Now that I have proved many of your turns,'[1] said Gamelin, 'you must prove one or two of mine.' With that he went briskly in to his antagonist, and of all the turns he was master of he showed him but one. He threw him on his left side, and broke three of his ribs: his left arm too gave a great crack. 'Shall it hold for a cast or not?' said the youth gaily. 'Whatever it be,' replied the other, 'he that comes under your hand shall not escape.'

Then the Franklin, who had lost his two sons, blessed the conqueror, and jeeringly told the champion he had been taught how to play; who, liking nothing at that time passing well, pronounced Gamelin to be master of them all,

---

[1] Turn—a sleight in wrestling.

and his play to be fatal. 'Since first I wrestled, (now yore ago) I never was so handled as to-day.'

The young champion now stood alone in the place, fearless, and cried, 'If there be any more, let them come to work; for my fellow here, judging by his countenance, does not seem desirous to go on.' But not one answered the challenge when they beheld his rough handling. Two gentlemen, owners of the place, then came forward, and told him to put on his hose and shoes, for that the fair was over. Yet Gamelin wished to continue, 'for,' said he, 'I have not half sold my ware.'—'He is a fool who buys of you,' replied the conquered champion, 'for you sell your wares so dear.'—'Why do you want so much of his goods?' said the Franklin, 'by St. James, you have bought them a great deal too cheap.' Then the wardens came forth and brought Gamelin the prize ram and the ring; and in the morning he set forwards to his home with joy and triumph.

His brother saw him coming with all the crowd, and ordered the porter to shut the gate and keep him outside. So, when he arrived and found the door fastened, he told the fellow to open it and let in many a good man's son. The hireling, however, insolently refused, and swore he should not enter the yard. 'You lie!' said Gamelin; and with that word he smote the wicket with his foot, and broke away the bolt. When the porter saw it might be no better, he set foot to earth and fled away as fast as he could. But Gamelin was as light of foot as he, and having overtaken him, he girt him full upon the neck and broke the bone. Then with the same arm he took up the carcass and threw it into a deep well. The other servants in the yard made off, dreading his vengeance and the company he had brought with him.

Afterwards he threw wide open the gates, and welcomed his attendants, saying, 'We will be masters here, and ask no man's leave. It was but yesterday that I left in my brother's cellars five tuns of right good wine, and we will not part company while a sup remains. And if my brother grudge, or make us a foul cheer, I am the caterer, and for his grudging he shall have our holy Lady's curse. He is but a niggard, and we will spend largely what he has hoarded. And whoever else here dares gainsay our will, shall keep company with the porter.'

Seven days and seven nights Gamelin held his feast, and all the while his brother lay close in a little turret, seeing him waste his goods, and feared to speak.

Early on the morning of the eighth day the guests prepared to depart from their host, who grieved that they should go before the wine was spent; but they bade him farewell, and went their way. All the while he was in possession of the store, his brother thought how he could wreak upon him his treachery. So, when the guests had left, Gamelin stood alone, and without a friend: and, shortly after, he was taken by surprise, and bound. Then came the false Knight from his hiding place, and, drawing near to his brother, asked who made him so bold as to waste and destroy his store? 'Brother,' answered Gamelin, 'spare your wrath; for many a day since, the whole was purchased with my money. Fifteen ploughs of land have you had for full sixteen years; and of all the beasts you have bred, that my father bequeathed to me, I give you the profit for the meat and drink hat we have now spent.'

'Hearken, then, brother Gamelin,' said the false Knight, 'what I will give you. Since I have no heir, I will make you the heir of my whole possession.' The guileless youth, not suspecting his brother, yielded to his terms.

'One thing, then, I must needs tell you,' said he; 'when you threw my porter into the well, I vowed in my wrath that you should be bound both hand and foot. Let me not, therefore, I beseech you, brother Gamelin, be foresworn; but consent to be confined, only for the maintenance of my oath.'

'You shall not be foresworn for me,' replied the youth: so they bound him hand and foot, and the Knight, knowing and fearing his strength, added great fetters to the bonds. They fastened him to a post in the hall, and the Knight told those who came in and looked upon him, that he was mad.

'Now, by my head brother,' said Gamelin, 'I see that you are a false one.' And when he had remained there two days and two nights, without food, he said at last to Adam le Dispenser,[1] 'Adam, I have fasted over long; I

[1] The dispenser was the steward of the store-room.

beseech you, therefore, of the great love which my father bore you, if you can come by the keys, that you will release me from bondage, and I will divide my inheritance with you.'

Adam Spenser answered him, ' I have served your brother full sixteen years, and if I were to set you free, he would afterwards account me traitor.'

' Adam,' said Gamelin, ' by my head, shall prove my brother at the last to be righ false. Loosen me, therefore, out of prison, and I will part with you my own free lands.'

' Upon so good a promise,' said he, ' I will do all that in me lies.'

' As you hold by me, I will maintain my covenant with you,' said Gamelin.

Anon after this, when his Lord had gone to bed, Adam took the keys and set him free. He loosed him hand and foot, hoping for the advancement that he had been promised.

' Heaven be praised,' said Gamelin, ' now am I at liberty. Had I but eaten and drank a meal, there is none in this house that should bind me to-night.'

Then Adam took him hastily, and as still as

a stone, to the store-room, and set him blithely at his supper. When he had eaten well, and drunk well too of the red wine, 'Adam,' said he, 'give me now your advice, shall I go and strike off my brother's head?'

'No,' said the other, 'I will give you counsel worth two of that. On Sunday we are to have a feasting of Abbots and Priors, and many other holy churchmen. You shall stand up by the post as before, bound hand and foot, and I will leave your fetters unlocked, that you may cast them off at will. When they have finished eating, and washed their hands, you shall bespeak them all to release you from your bonds: and if they become your security, so much the better fare; you will be out of prison, and I out of blame. But if each of them deny us, then do I swear to do another thing. You shall have a good staff, and I will have one too; and evil befall him who is untrue to the other.'

'And if I fail on my side,' said Gamelin, 'evil attend me. So, do you give me warning when to begin, and we will assoil them of their sins.'

'When I wink at you,' answered Adam, 'look

to be off; cast away your fetters, and come straight to me.'

'Bless your bones, Adam, but that is right good advice. Only let them refuse to free me from prison, and I will handsomely pound their loins.'

The Sunday came, and all the folks sat down to the feast. As each passed in at the hall door, he cast an eye upon Gamelin; for they had been set against him by the foul slander of his brother, the Knight. And when they had been served with two or three messes, the prisoner called aloud, 'In what manner have I been provided? Is it well that I should sit here fasting, while others, in my own home, are taking their fill, and making glad?' Then the false Knight told them all that he was a madman. But Gamelin remained still and answered nothing, for he held all Adam's words in his thought. Some time after he dolefully implored the great Lords, who were sitting there in hall, to help him out of his bondage: and one of the Abbots answered, 'Ill betide the man who shall become your pledge, and release you from prison; and all worship wait upon him, who shall meet you with sorrow.' A second wished his head were off, although he were his own brother. A third—a Prior, said that it was a great sorrow and care to have him alive.

'On—on!' said young Gamelin: 'so is my petition broken;—now have I found out that I have no friends in the world. May no good follow him, who would bestow any upon Abbots or Priors.'

Adam had now taken away the cloth, and watching his young master, saw that his rage was running high; so thinking, at that time, little about the pantry, he brought two good stakes to the hall door, and looked the signal to Gamelin, who threw off his fetters, and walked forth. Then Gamelin, with Adam Spenser by his side came into the hall, and, looking fiercely round, both set to work. The one sprinkled the holy water with his good oak cudgel, and many a one bowed to the dispensation; some to the ground; others tumbled into the fire: Abbot and Prior, Monk and Canon, all that he overtook felt his supremacy; and not one of the hirelings the while, who waited in the hall, wished him any thing but good; so they stood by, and let the two work on, for none had pity on the churchmen. All who came within reach of Gamelin's staff he overthrew, and was quit of his debt. 'Pay them good wages,' said Adam, 'for love of me; I will guard the door, and may I never hear mass again, if any go out unassoiled.'

'Doubt nothing,' said Gamelin, 'while we hold together; you keep well the door, and I will work here.'

'Do them every thing but good,' rejoined Adam, 'for they are churchmen;—draw no blood from them—save their crowns, but crack their arms and legs.' So Gamelin and Adam played away upon the Monks, and made them all aghast; and they who had come riding there jollily were carried home again in carts and waggons. 'Alas! alas! my lord Abbot,' said a grey Friar, 'what did we do here? We had better have been at home with our bread and water.'

All this while the Knight remained quite still, and made a dismal appearance. Then Gamelin up with his staff, and by one blow on

THE COOK'S TALE OF GAMELIN.

'All who came within reach of Gamelin's staff he overthrew, and was quit of his debt.'

his neck upset him; and ended with laying him in the same fetters, where he had been before. 'Sit you there, my brother John,' said he, 'and cool your hot blood, as I did mine.'

After they had well finished their task with their enemies, they asked for water to wash themselves; and all the servants yielded obedience, some for love and some for fear.

The Sheriff, who lived about five miles off, was quickly told how Gamelin and Adam had bound and wounded many persons, against the King's peace. Strife awoke at the outrage, and he was casting about to take the author of it, when a score of bold young fellows came to the Sheriff, and gained his leave to bring them away by force. They started off at full speed, nor once rested till they arrived at the house: and when they knocked at the gate, the porter who served Gamelin with loving faithfulness, looked slily out of a hole at them for a little time, and dreading some treachery, kept the wicket fast, and asked their will. One only of the company spoke, desiring that they should be let in.— 'Before I do that, I must know your errand,' said the porter. 'Then tell Adam and Gamelin that we would speak two or three words with them.'—'You stand quietly there, then,' said the Porter, 'and I will go and know his will.' He went to his master and warned him that his enemies were without. 'The Sheriff's men, Sir,' said he, 'are now all at the gate to take you both; you cannot escape!' Gamelin answered him, 'My good porter, as I may prosper you, I will allow your words when I see my time for it.' Then turning to Adam, 'Look to be gone—enemies are at the gate; the Sheriff's men have come, and sworn together to take us.'—'Go forth briskly,' said Adam, 'and evil follow me if I leave you this day. We will so welcome these Sheriff-fellows, that some of them, I guess, will make their beds in the fen.'

So the two, with each a good sturdy quarter-staff in hand, went out of the postern gate, and began laying about them; Adam felled his two, and Gamelin brought three to the ground; the rest set foot to earth, and began to scour off. 'Hollo!' said Adam, 'stay and take a cup of wine with us.'—'No—no,' said they, 'we don't like your drink; it will lay a man's brains in his hood.'

Then Gamelin stood still, and looking about him, saw the Sheriff coming with a great crowd. 'We must stay here no longer,' said he, 'unless we would have ugly fare. It is better to be at liberty in the woods than bound in a town.' So each took the other's hand, and drank a draught of wine together, and afterwards pursued their course. The Sheriff came up and found the nest, but the birds had flown. So he alighted, and went into the hall, where the Lord lay fettered, whom he released, and after sent for a surgeon to come and heal his wound. And here we will leave the false Knight, lying in trouble, and look after Gamelin, to see how he fares.

The outcast wandered, in silence, about the wild wood, and Adam little liked the prospect before them; but thought it was a merrier thing to be a dispenser. 'Now,' said he, 'would I much rather be handling my keys, than walking up and down these woods, and tearing my clothes.'

'Do not be cast down, Adam,' replied his friend, 'many a good man's child is brought into trouble.'

While they were talking in an under-breath, they heard voices near to them; and looking below the boughs, perceived full seven score young men, well clad, all seated at meat. 'Now, cast aside all your doubts,' said Gamelin; 'help comes after sorrow, and if I see right, there is good meat and drink.' Adam looked under the bough, and was glad enough when he surely saw the fare, for sorely did he long after a good meal. Just at that moment, the master of the band noticed the two, standing under the shaw,[1] and desired his men to go and bring them to him, that he might enquire who they were. And quickly at the word, seven started up from their dinner, and coming near to the wanderers, claimed that they should yield their bows and arrows. 'Sorrow be to them,' said Gamelin, 'who yield to you; though you may fetch five more, and then there will be twelve of you.' They thought by his speech that he could trust in

[1] Shaw: a shade of trees.

the strength of his arm; not one, therefore, came forth to make the trial: but all mildly entreated him to come before their master, and tell his will. 'Upon your loyalty, young man,' said Gamelin to one of the company, 'tell me who is your master?' All of them answered him sincerely, 'Our master is the crowned king of the outlaws.' Then said Gamelin to Adam, 'Go we, in heaven's name; he cannot, for shame, refuse us meat and drink: and if he be courteous, and come of gentle blood, we shall fare well.' 'By St. James,' answered Adam, 'whatever harm I get, I will adventure to the very door, for some food.'

So both went forth together, and greeted the master of the band; who asked of them what they were seeking, under the woody shaws. 'He must needs walk the forest,' said young Gamelin, 'who dare not keep the town. Sir, we design no harm here, unless peradventure to shoot the deer we may meet, as men who are hungry, and have no food, and are hard bestead in the forest wilds.' Then the master had pity on him for his words, and told the two to sit down, and fare of the best.

While they were eating, it became known to one and another, that their new guest was young Gamelin. So the master was summoned to council, and the thing was told to him: whereupon the new outlaw was made master of the troop under their king.

Within the third week after this, tidings came to the head master that he might return home, for that his peace was made: upon which young Gamelin was crowned King of the Outlaws, in his place; and for a while he held sway under the woody shaws.

The false Knight, his brother, was now created Sheriff, and through hatred and revenge, he issued out an indictment against him. Then were all the bondmen of the Knight sorry, that the hue and cry of 'Wolf's Head'[1] should be proclaimed against their young Lord, and they sent messengers to seek him in the wilds, and inform him of the event; also that all his goods were forfeit and taken away, and

---

[1] This term evidently took its origin from the well-known proclamation of King Edgar, who, to clear the country of wolves, set a price upon every head that should be brought into the hundred or tithing court.

his hirelings scattered. 'Alas!' said Gamelin, 'that my hand was so slack, as not to have broken his neck. Go, and tell all my friends, that as God shall have my life, so will I be present at the next county meeting.'

True to his appointment, he came boldly into the hall, and courteously putting aside his hood, greeted the Lords assembled;—'but as for you—broken-back Sheriff,—evil be your portion!—Why have you done that shame and villainy, as to send forth against me the wolf's-head hue and cry?' The other made no reply, but ordered him to be seized, and thrown into prison, where he was heavily fettered.

Gamelin had a brother, named Sir Ote, a courteous and good man. A messenger came, and informed him altogether, how evilly the youngest of his mother's sons was used. The gentle Knight was grieved at the news, and quickly saddling his horse, came straight to his two brothers. 'Sir,' said he to the Sheriff, 'there be only three of us, and you have imprisoned the best of all. Evil follow such a brother as you are!'

'Sir Ote,' said the false Knight, 'spare your curses, for he shall only fare the worse for your big words. He has been legally taken to the King's gaol, and there he shall remain till the Judge arrives.'

'But,' said the other, 'it were better to bail him; I therefore require that you take my pledge for his deliverance at the next session, and then let Gamelin fairly stand his chance.'

'Brother,' said the Knight, 'I take your promise; and by the soul of my father, if he be not ready to appear when the court is sitting, you shall endure the penalty of the sentence.'

The two parties agreed to the terms proposed, when Gamelin was delivered to Sir Ote, and that night both dwelt together.

On the morrow Gamelin desired to go and see how his company fared in the woods.— 'Nay then,' said Sir Ote, 'I now see that all the care will fall on my own head: for if you be not found when the Judge is sitting, I shall be taken, and shall suffer in your place.'— 'Brother,' said Gamelin, 'be not afraid to trust me; for, by St. James, if God do but grant me life and wit, I will be ready in court when the Judge arrives.'—' God shield you from shame, Gamelin, my brother,' said the good Knight, ' come when you see the fit time, and bring us out of reproach.' So the young outlaw went his way to the free woods, where he found all his young men, to whom he related how he had been bound; and they in return, recounted to him their adventures during his thraldom. All the while that Gamelin was an outlaw, no man fared the worse for his deeds; no curse clave to him, except it were that of the Abbots, Priors, and all the fraternity of Monks: with them, indeed, he left naught that could be reft away. So he and his jolly company carried on their game of free booty, and mirth grew rife among them; but at the same time, the false Knight was plying every art to gain over the jury, that he might hang his brother.

At length, on a certain day, as Gamelin stood and surveyed the shadowy woods within the wild field, he thought upon Sir Ote, his good brother, how that he had promised him to be ready when the Justice was seated, and that he would, without more delay, hold his word, and come up to judgment. He therefore told his young men to be prepared quickly, for that he must needs go, or his brother, who had become bail for him, would be thrown into prison. So he, and all his bold compeers, came away to the town, where they found that the false Knight had basely suborned the jury to condemn whichever brother might be brought before them. 'The court is seated, Adam,' said Gamelin, 'do you go in and see what process they make.' He went, and soon returned, bringing word that he saw the space filled with great Lords and stout, and his brother, Sir Ote, standing in the midst of the court, fettered. 'God grant us success in our undertaking,' said the young chieftain, 'and he shall sorely abide who brought my brother to that pass.'—'Then,' said Adam, 'if you will follow my advice, there is not one in that hall who shall bear away his head.'—'Not so, Adam,' answered his Lord, 'we will slay the guilty only, and let the rest go free. I will myself go into the hall and hear the cause go on; and woe betide the doers of false judgment. Let none escape at the door, for I will be Justice to-day, and award the doom. Heaven speed me in this my new work! Adam, you shall come with me, and be my clerk of the court.' His men all promised to do their best, and be at hand should he need their help: 'For we will stand by you so long as we may endure, and if we work not mainly, pay us no wages.'—'As ye abide by me, so shall you find me a trusty master,' said Gamelin. So when the whole Court were assembled, in he went, and boldly stood amongst them all.

First he unfettered his brother Sir Ote, who said, 'Gamelin, you have staid away almost too long, for the quest has gone out against me that I should be hanged.'

'Brother,' said Gamelin, 'Heaven grant me success, but this good day they who have been upon your trial shall themselves suffer a felon's death; both they and the Judge, together with our brother, for through him all this began.'

Then said the youth to that false Judge, 'Arise, and void your place,—your power is at an end: you have given an unjust doom; I, therefore, will take your place, and set all right.' But the Judge kept his seat and would not arise for his words; when Gamelin with his sword clave his cheek bone, and after seizing him in his arms, without any more speech threw him over the bar and broke his worship's arm. No one dared say aught but good to Gamelin, for fear of the great company who stood without the doors. He then sat down in the judgment seat, Sir Ote was at his side, and Adam took his place at his footstool.

First he ordered the Judge and his false brother to be placed side by side at the bar; after which he made enquiry who were upon the quest to doom that his good brother should be hanged: and when they were pointed out, he ordered them all to be fettered and placed also at the bar. Then, addressing himself to the unrighteous Judge, he told him that he had passed a foul and unlawful sentence: 'you and the twelve jurymen,' said he, 'shall certainly be hanged this day.' The Sheriff now began piteously to entreat his mercy, and to call to mind that he was his brother. 'And, therefore,' said Gamelin, 'may evil dog your footsteps; had you been master still, I should have fared the worse.'

To make short my tale, he ordained a jury of his own strong young fellows; and, at their sentence, the Judge and Sheriff, together with the twelve jurymen, were all hanged up, and left to wave and dry in the wind.

So ended the false and treacherous life of the Knight; and this was his father's curse, which followed him to the last.

Sir Ote was now the eldest, and Gamelin still young; so, with their friends they went to court, and made their peace with the King. The King loved Sir Ote well, and made him a Justice of Assize; and Gamelin he ordained head warden of all his free forests. The act of outlawry passed against his young men was repealed, and all were appointed to good offices about the Court.

And so young Gamelin regained all his lands, and quitted himself with his enemies. Sir Ote also made him his heir, and afterwards our hero married a good and fair wife, with whom he lived in bliss till he was gathered to mother earth. And all here shall do the like—no man may escape. May our Lord bring us to that joy which endureth for evermore.

LONDON: PRINTED BY
SPOTTISWOODE AND CO., NEW-STREET SQUARE
AND PARLIAMENT STREET